OUTDOOR ADVERTISING

HISTORY AND REGULATION

edited by

JOHN W. HOUCK

UNIVERSITY OF

NOTRE DAME PRESS — 1969

Notre Dame   *London*

CONTENTS

ACKNOWLEDGEMENT

Acknowledgement must be made, and gratefully, to the Outdoor Advertising Foundation here at Notre Dame's College of Business Administration; Outdoor Advertising Institute of America and its president, Frank Cawl, Jr., and vice-president, Ann Noonan; Bureau of Public Roads, Department of Transportation, Washington, D.C., *Signs of Our Time,* Cincinnati; Burkhart Advertising, and its president, Charles Burkhart. Personal thanks to my colleagues, Dean Thomas T. Murphy, John Malone, and my chairman, Salvatore Bella. To Miss Emily Schossberger, the Director of the University of Notre Dame Press, to my editor, an editor's editor, who believed in the importance of this book's theme, Dominic Lorenzo, Associate Director of the University of Notre Dame Press; to my student secretary, Richard DeSimon; and to my wife, Mary Dooley Houck. Finally, a sense of gratitude for Mrs. Lyndon B. Johnson, who made the beautification of America her personal commitment.

John W. Houck

*   *   *

Mr. Phillip Tocker acknowledges with gratitude the valued assistance of Karl Ghaster, Jr., formerly Vice-President of the OAAA.

I. TOWARD A SOCIETY OF VISUAL QUALITY

John W. Houck

"America the Beautiful," a patriotic hymn, may become an ironic dirge, a remembrance of what once was America, or of what could have been America. Either way we face a crisis in visual environment in our cities, suburbs and on our highways. Old neighborhoods, architecturally, aesthetically, or quaintly worth saving, are allowed to decline. We build functional (with little amenity) canyons of steel and glass that repel us because of their sameness. We allow the wasting away of "downtowns" (even in their prime these left much to be desired) to be replaced by gaudy shopping centers. Strips of stores, drive-ins and gasoline alleys stretch through our cities, suburbs and out to our rural areas. All compete for the motorist's dollar by larger and larger on-premise signs and shield the viewer from the cinder-block banality of most of our commercial buildings. We have saved Grand Canyon for that 1 percent of our population who go there for one week in the summer, but we have condemned the remaining 99 percent to an increasing lack of beauty, charm, variety and amenity in our cities and suburbs.

Urban America is many things: it is functional; it is rich; it is mobile. But is it beautiful? I think not, and the likelihood of reversing the uglification of America is small. Whether we move toward a society of visual beauty depends on how deeply and quickly we become committed to this ideal. It also depends on whether the structures, streets, roads, downtowns, new suburbs and industrial areas, all built to last thirty years or more, will stand the test of aesthetic judgment over those years and beyond—into the twenty-first century.

America of the Future will be visually what we build and also what we save from the past. For what we save from the past will provide us with a much needed variety and charm. The great old houses, the shops and odd hotels somehow must be preserved from the wrecking cranes and the financial calculations of the real estate developers. It gives stridency to this theme when we recall how close Lafayette Square (in front of the White House) came to losing all its historic charm, when it was proposed to replace the old townhouses with new buildings. We need to save much to retain a sense of our history (short as it may be) and to give us a future of variety. This sense of our past will help to moderate the immediacy of current problems, giving us a much needed perspective.

This series of essays is committed to exploring the accommodation of two societal interests—highway beautification and outdoor advertising. And we believe that an accommodation is possible, though we, as a society, are still dickering over the price. But we delude ourselves if we seek an accommodation that fits for a 1965 America and not for a 1980 America or a 1990 or beyond.

Let me try to explain. Our accommodation of 1965,[1] unless we change it, was programmed for at least 1973 and, if I am right about the stretch-out because of the war, will have to do for 1980. Or to put it succinctly, 1980 America will be governed by a 1965 accommodation; instead of 1965 accommodation being governed by the projected needs of 1980.

To remedy this disparity, I suggest that we as a society must accept the necessity of living in the future *right now,* and reject a type of bifurcation view which is too compartmentalized and will not do the job adequately. The present with all its demands will win out over the future,

[1] One of the happier by-products of our Vietnam involvement, I suggest, is a slow-down in the administration of the Highway Beautification Act of 1965, with its control of outdoor advertising and junkyards and its provision for landscaping and scenic enhancement on federal-aid highways.

which, we sometimes blindly think, can be put off or ignored, but which really cannot be. A better interpretation of the concept, "to live in the future right now," is that of a continuum. The important characteristic is the lack of any distinction between present and future. Of course, this is not a new idea; what is new is our growing awareness and confidence in living and planning the future right now. Too often societies have been only *past* oriented. The new intellectual tools (and material surplus) give us the base for the shift from past-present orientation to a past-present-future orientation. Certainly there is a new confidence in our intellectual tools:

1. Recent growth of social technologies[2] (sociology, psychology, economics, administrative sciences, law, to name a few) that can bring our social knowledge into parity with the physical sciences and technologies.

2. A conceptual shift by some intellectuals from a past-present orientation, with its emphasis on understanding what-can't-be-changed-only-better-known, to a past-present-future orientation, with its emphasis on shaping what can be changed in human affairs. De Jouvenel writes in the book *The Art of Conjecture,* "For man in his role as an active agent the future is a field of liberty and power, but for man in his role as a cognizant being the future is a field of uncertainty."

3. Recent achievements of "social engineering" suggest *some* optimism about our intellectual and social methodologies:
   a) our mastery of economic depressions and extreme business cycles,
   b) our management of such weapons as nuclear bombs and missiles for almost a quarter of a century without full-scale war,
   c) the recovery from World War II devastation in Europe and Asia.

[2] Olaf Helmer's phrase. See his volume *Social Technology* (New York: Basic Books, Inc., 1966).

4. An embryonal awareness that single-purpose planning, presently characteristic of business firms and political units, will not suffice and that such an approach leaves us with many newly discovered problems as we become more sensitive and more sophisticated.

"Single-purpose planning calculates only the immediate intended effect of proposed projects; it fails to account for the total environmental impact. . . . Ways must be found to move toward a concept of multi-purpose planning that recognizes the full spectrum of human needs. This kind of planning would require broad research to determine precisely what those needs are and how priorities among them are to be allocated."[3]

Whether this intellectual phenomenon, the way we plan and build our society for the future, is spreading fast enough and deep enough is another question. Though I might suggest a negative answer, I think it is a debatable point. I am sure of this: the options open to our children and grandchildren are what we do or fail to do; future America, at least much of it, is being made right now.

How do we live in the future *right now?* It is, I suggest, a matter of three steps:

First, a projection or prediction of the major determinants of our society, for let us say, the year 2000 has to be made. Many people will gag at the effrontery of attempting such long-range forecasting when our success with much shorter periods, like next year's GNP or the anticipated cost of Medicare, seem to be so far off the mark. However, long-range forecasting does not have to be as accurate as short-range projections. Next year's GNP forecast will tell us how much we can spend and how much we should tax or borrow; if we are off, we will know it soon. All kinds of policy decisions will be taken on this forecast; whether it be 830 billion or 860 billion, a difference of less than 4

[3] Harold Gilliam, in *Daedalus, The Journal of the American Academy of Arts and Sciences,* Fall 1967, p. 1143.

percent, will dictate much of vital monetary and fiscal policy, foreign and domestic policy, for our society. But if the range of forecast for our population in the year 2000 is from 320 to 360 million, either the low or high estimate signals that much must be done to prepare ourselves to provide adequately for these increments in population. We do not need precision to be alerted for long-range planning.

The following forecast by Herman Kahn and Anthony J. Wiener, appearing in the Summer 1967 issue of *Daedalus,* confronts some of these details. I have selected this forecast, because it deals directly with urbanization, highways and land-use, subjects appropriate to this volume.

> The United States in the year 2000 will probably see at least three gargantuan megalopolises. We have labeled these—only half-frivolously—"Boswash," "Chipitts," and "Sansan." Boswash identifies the megalopolis that will extend from Washington to Boston (something under 80 million people). Chipitts, concentrated around the Great Lakes, may stretch from Chicago to Pittsburgh and north to Canada—thereby including Detroit, Toledo, Cleveland, Akron, Buffalo, and Rochester. This megalopolis seems likely to contain more than one-eighth of the U.S. population (perhaps 40 million people or more). Sansan, a Pacific megalopolis that will presumably stretch from Santa Barbara (or even San Francisco) to San Diego, should contain more than one-sixteenth of the population (perhaps 20 million people or more) . . . The three megalopolises should contain roughly one half of the total U.S. population, including the overwhelming majority of the most technologically and scientifically advanced, and prosperous intellectual and creative elements. Even Sansan will have a larger total income than all but five or six nations. Study of the U.S. in the year 2000 may largely be of Boswash, Chipitts, and Sansan.[4]

[4] *Daedalus,* Summer 1967, pp. 718/719.

These two gentlemen go on to forecast a GNP range of 1.5 trillion dollars to 4 trillion dollars, or a per capita income range of about 5,000 to 15,000 dollars, in 1965 dollars, though they suggest that the higher GNP and per capita income is the likelier. To sum this up: a large increase in population, centered in three megalopolises, with a per capita income in 1965 dollars of about three times what it is today, or 12,000 dollars—all of this in the year 2000.

The mind boggles at these aggregates: where are these 140 million to live? What is the impact on the values and attitudes of our population with so much communal and per capita wealth? What do these mega-lopolises mean, as compared to our present urban areas? Will these people be happy? Materially happy? Emotionally happy? Without very good answers to any of these questions, we must somehow plan for these increments and aggregates. We can do this only by adopting the technique of science, breaking down the unmanageable whole into more manageable parts. It is beyond the scope of this paper to elaborate on the complexity of both analysis and subsequent synthesis needed to do the job. But some further refinements of the problems, suggested by Kahn and Wiener, are needed to fill out the mosaic of the future. Certainly three areas of interest to this volume need to be highlighted:

1. We will probably have double or more the number of automobiles that we presently have. This predication has great ramifications on how our cities, highways, freeways, suburbs and countryside will develop.

> When the present 70 million cars go to 100 million in 1980, many a city will look like the still of a giant ant heap. Some do already. Cities are becoming suburbia's mammoth garages as well as its crossways. Los Angeles—"The freeway city"—is already using two-thirds of its downtown area for freeways, streets, and off-street parking, and America's current car pilots are only the out riders of the invasion to come.[5]

[5] Charles Abrams, *The City Is the Frontier* (New York, Harpers, 1965), p. 326.

Most of what is populated America today looks as it does because of the mobility of our society. The immense amount of concrete covering our cities, the many roads and freeways, the ribbonlike commercial areas that stretch for miles, the growth of the suburbs—all are the results of the automobile's capacity to make travel cheap and individualized. What we see, and therefore judge to be beautiful or ugly, is what we see from a moving vehicle. Or if we are walking through a commercial area, on one side is moving traffic or parked cars and on the other, business (too often) competing to catch the attention of the motorist. Therefore, any attempt to beautify urban America must encompass the fact and requirements of growing numbers of automobiles. We may be defeated before we start or we may have to take up the spirit of Mr. Bosselman's proposal about signs being example of pop art—a thing of beauty—and learn to appreciate cars as works of art or the equivalent of shrubs or trees, millions of them.

Another effect of the automobile on our society (as well as population growth and megalopolis-building) is the loss of community identity. If Kahn and Wiener are right about urban clustering into megalopolises, what will be the response when one is asked: "Where do you come from—Chipitts, Boswash or Sansan?" Will there still be a sense of belonging to a community with its history, tradition and variety? For instance the old Main Street could become the modern Interstate Highway System connecting the many populated areas of the megalopolis of Chipitts. What will happen to such "towns" as Toledo, Elkhart, South Bend, Gary or Racine? There is strong possibility of a net loss in civic pride and culture that contributed so much in the past to building these communities. This possibility not only affects the inhabitant's sense of well-being attained by growing up in an identifiable community, but also the thousands of citizens whose voluntary services made these communities better places in which to live and work.

Because of mass production, mass consumption, mass media and instant tract-housing, we confront the real danger of the complete homogenization of American culture. Will we lose the variety that is an outgrowth of our many cities and their histories? The many industries and commercial activities, the old rich and new rich, cultural and educational attainments, different periods of architecture (post-Civil War, turn-of-the-century, 1920's)—these variables contribute to making one city different from another. As a friend remarked after flying to a wedding in a suburb outside St. Louis: "The airport, motels, freeways, suburbs and even church architecture seemed to be the same as other cities. I could have been in Dallas or Los Angeles or Chicago." We will be miles ahead of the rest of the world in creature comforts, but we will have paid a price by the loss of variety and personal identification.

2. Any attempt to enhance the beauty of the United States, outside publicly owned lands, brings us face to face with the concept of private property. For instance, the 1965 Highway Beautification Act severely limited the "right" of businessmen to put up highway signs on private land adjacent to public highways. Even by present property-law standards, this is considered a radical change. Mr. David Gooder, counsel for the Outdoor Advertising Association of America, Inc., at the Notre Dame conference on highway beautification stated:

> Some of the strongest arguments against governmental land planning stem from norms prescribing freedom for the private property owner in our society . . . . We depend upon private land development. Why? Because we suspect that no one has a monopoly on the true and the beautiful, that if you give a governmental agency a monopoly on decision-making you do not get as good decisions as you do if you leave it to a multitude of individuals. I don't say unlimited freedom of property, after all we have had local zoning for decades, but very little should be put in government's hands . . . .

The small motel owner, for instance, is dependent on signs to pull in the traffic, unlike the large motel chains. If you remove his signs, you remove him, and he can't live on experiments about new ways of reaching the traffic. . . .

Historically, the arguments that Mr. Gooder raised are classified in property law under the general theme: how much of a public interest is there in private property. This problem was not crucial when we had land to spare and most of our people lived on farms. Nor was it a problem when our dominant drive was exploitation of the land to eke out a living for our people. We do not now have land to spare, at least where people apparently want to live. Our people overwhelmingly live in city and suburb. And we are a long way from bare subsistence, and if Kahn and Wiener's forecast hits anywhere near the mark, we are on the way to three times our present per capita wealth. This tremendous increment in wealth may mean very likely greater leisure, education and the resources to enjoy the "finer things of life."

It is a fundamental postulate of most critics of our highways (including this writer) that the present gaudy disorder along them cannot lay claim to inclusion among the "finer things of life." And if there is not *now* a consensus as to this judgment, there will be, as the gaudiness expands and our people grow in sophistication. This means a greater public interest in visual quality as it relates to private uses of land. What a property owner does on his land may create a visual nuisance for neighboring landowners and for the general public and must be dealt with by a public agency. The conflict of public interests and private rights over the same piece of property that is exposed to the general public will shift more and more toward the public-interest side of the ledger.

3. When we look at the forecasted aggregates of a three- or four-trillion dollar GNP, and a per capita range up to about twelve thousand in 1965

dollars, it is easy to come to the conclusion that we will have plenty of dollars for beauty, amenity and charm. But do we? Aggregates cover two large classes of expenditures: communal-government and private-business. Both have to conform to some acceptable criteria; business demands a return on investment. Private expenditures are and will be the larger component, though we will be purchasing more communal goods, like clean air, unpolluted streams, public recreational areas, space-exploration and national defense.

But, if private business will be making the major decisions about what will be built, where and with what degree of beauty, how can business "budget" for beauty, charm and amenity? To some degree our forecasted three-times-our-present-per-capita-income will result in consumers demanding these qualities in some stores, hotels and restaurants. And businessmen will have to respond. And they will make money doing this. There will be, I suspect, large areas of lag and unevenness in the effort for visual quality. And there will also be great numbers of businessmen who will not be able to see that visual quality can be a profitable venture or socially necessary. We are left with the need to insist through regulation, or through some kind of grant-in-aid program, or possibly a mixture of the two techniques. We need a huge public-private corporation, modeled after the Ford Foundation, to encourage beauty in our visual environment.

As stated earlier "living in the future right now" is a matter of three steps if we are to build a society of visual quality. The first step is "playing" with the forecasts of the major determinants of the future society as best we can. The remaining two steps are to plan for a society we want and, finally, to get on with the labor of insuring that America will be beautiful in 1990 or 2001.

II. STANDARDIZED OUTDOOR ADVERTISING: HISTORY, ECONOMICS AND SELF-REGULATION

Phillip Tocker

ADVERTISING

Any reference to standardized outdoor advertising involves a comprehension quite different from that entertained by the public at large. This medium—available in more markets and exposed to more people than any of the other major advertising media—comprises only about 1 percent of all commercial signs, displays and devices visible to the public eye.

Advertising comes from two Latin words, "ad," meaning "toward," and "vertere," meaning "to turn." The objective of advertising can be explained by derivation, i.e., *"to turn"* the attention of any given market of buyers *"toward"* a product, service, idea, or personality.

Advertising is not a separate industry in the sense that steel, oil, food, construction and mining are industries. It is a tool, a technique or instrument used in many different fields for specialized purposes. Advertising is not an end in itself, nor is it a separate and independent function. It is an important part of marketing. As a force in our economy, it is vital to our free-market system. It affects consumption, production and investment. It informs, interprets, symbolizes, persuades and often entertains. As an instrument of business, it links buyers and sellers in a vast, efficient communications network. As such, advertising is the active voice and energetic servant of the American system of free enterprise.

*Early Examples of Electric On-Premise Signs That Lighted
Up Our City Streets*

Another Example of Electric Signs That Made "The Great White Way" Possible

Advertising is made up of two parts: what to say, and how to say it. It is the delivery, by a given medium or combination of media—the "how to say it,"—and the "what to say," to a *defined* audience in a *given* period of time.

In our dynamic and expanding economy, there are increasingly more products to market and more people to reach. Yet the advertising cost per capita has not significantly increased. In this sense, we can say that advertising is becoming more efficient.

Advertisers don't buy newspapers, magazines, TV, radio or billboards per se. They buy an audience and through advertising influence this audience. The average day of an American is usually divided into three parts: eight hours of work, eight hours of leisure, and eight hours of sleep. Since very few people are exposed to advertising during their work, and none are exposed to it during their sleep, advertising communication must reach them during their leisure hours or during time spent in travel to work, to shop, to school or for recreation.

OUTDOOR ADVERTISING

To most people, the term outdoor advertising is applied to many things —from the huge electric spectaculars in Times Square to the small store signs used by most merchants. Broadly defined, outdoor advertising consists of all forms of advertising which people are exposed to out-of-doors. Outdoor advertising has three unique characteristics:

1. It does not "circulate" a message to a market of buyers; the market "circulates" around the message.
2. Promotions are delivered to a moving audience that is actively trying to reach some destination.

3. Presentations must be made quickly as there is no time for detailed messages. It is estimated that six seconds is the average exposure of an individual to an outdoor message at one passing.

ON-PREMISE OUTDOOR ADVERTISING

There are two major classifications of outdoor advertising: on-premise and off-premise. The on-premise classification of outdoor advertising is referred to as the sign industry, in that signs are custom-made and are manufactured by a sign contractor on premises *not* owned, leased or controlled by the sign contractor or his agent. Such signs are used primarily for the purpose of identifying a business, its products or its services at the point of manufacture, distribution or sale, hence on-premise.

*Contemporary
On-Premise Sign*

Courtesy Signs of
Our Time

The enterprising merchant of ancient Babylonia is recorded as being among the first to realize the value of hanging a sign above his place of business to identify his trade or draw attention to his wares. However, it was not until the Roman Empire that the sign actually began to fill a widespread need. Since very few people could read or write, signs displayed all manner of animals and objects to catch the eye and inform the traveler—the bush for the tavern, the goat for the dairy, the knife for the cutler, and so on. However, as life progressed, more elaborate techniques were adopted. Throughout the major cities of Europe during

Pompeian Billboard

the 1300's, signs took on such importance that merchants and innkeepers were required by official edict to hang them on their establishments so that everybody could properly identify their businesses. The sign became, in effect, a man's license to do business. In the eighteenth century, talented coach-painters began turning their hands to sign painting, giving evidence that the sign could be a thing of beauty as well as of information. As a result, the streets of London and Paris soon became virtual art galleries.

With the approaching twentieth century came the prediction that "the electric sign was the sign of the future." The most practical incandescent electric lamp had already been developed and patented by Thomas Edison in 1879, and widespread use of the electric light was greeted

This Combination of Technology and Commercial Advertising Literally Changed the Cityscape of New York at Night

with enthusiasm in America. Cities acquired a dramatic and sparkling new beauty at night. The man who had a product to sell or a service to render was quick to recognize the many advantages of an illuminated sign. The electric sign industry was born.

In the United States, there are approximately 11,700 sign manufacturers, contractors and distributors. The majority of the operators in the sign industry are members of one or more of the following national trade associations: the National Electric Sign Association, the Advertising Metal Sign and Display Manufacturers Association and the Porcelain Enamel Institute. The signs installed by the sign industry are erected and maintained under lease or consent of the owner of the property on which they are placed and in accordance with the building code and/or sign ordinance of the related municipality.

The sign industry consists of two major divisions: electric and luminescent tube signs in retail or wholesale quantities, and commercial and point-of-purchase signs of any material in retail or wholesale quantities.[1]

OFF-PREMISE OUTDOOR ADVERTISING

Off-premise outdoor advertising is an advertising service for others which erects and maintains outdoor advertising displays on premises owned, leased or controlled by the producer of the advertising service. Off-premise outdoor advertising is comprised of two classifications: the rural roadside sign, and the urban-marketplace medium.

[1] The following data represents a conservative industry estimate for 1965:

Electric Signs		Commercial Signs	
Number of Displays	7,100,000	Number of Displays	16,900,000
Number of Companies	4,300	Number of Companies	7,400
Number of Employees	54,500	Number of Employees	10,000
Annual Sales	$740,000,000	Annual Sales Volume	$185,000,000

One of the First "Electric Spectaculars"

Traffic movements focus primarily on the central city and diminish rapidly on the fringes of urbanization. Thus, most of the traffic movements found within the urban area are the significant part of the central city market audience group. Such urban traffic movements can be referred to as "in-market traffic" and represent the audience target of the urban-marketplace medium.

Beyond the fringes of urbanization and in the rural area, traffic movements consist primarily of traffic socially and economically oriented to the trading area and "out-of-market traffic" involving travel over longer

This Example of a Painted Bulletin Spectacular Shows Some of the Steps in Rubber Tire Making

distances—travel between competitive markets, out-of-state and a substantial volume of commercial trucks. Since the "out-of-market" traffic is relatively foreign to a given urban area, there is a need for communication to orient highway users to the availability of such immediate roadside services as food, fuel and lodging. It is the function of the "roadside sign" to service this particular audience, the out-of-market traffic. As such, the "roadside sign" is primarily local and is generally geared to the *immediate* and *specific* needs of the traveling public. Approximately 50 percent of the display units are owned by the advertiser. In the general absence of zoning and building code authority in the rural areas, such signs are subject seldom to local regulation but to general state regulation.[2]

A Very Popular Advertisement

[2] The following data represents a conservative estimate of the economics of the rural roadside sign business for 1965:

| Number of Displays | 800,000 | Number of Employees | 9,000 |
| Number of Companies | 1,000 | Annual Sales | $250,000,000 |

There are three categories of off-premise advertising that service the urban marketplace. The first two, transit advertising and neighborhood point-of-purchase, are relatively small in volume of business. The third is the standardized medium of outdoor advertising.

Companies engaged in transit advertising provide space on or in public transit vehicles. This includes subway car cards, subway station posters, bus car cards, outside bus posters, taxicab cards, commuter train cards, floor exhibits and diorama displays at train and airline terminals.[3]

"Neighborhood point-of-purchase" is an auxiliary form of outdoor advertising. It consists of 3-sheet posters, 9 inches high by 5 feet wide or the more commonly used 6-sheet poster, 6 feet high by 12 feet long. These displays are generally affixed to the walls of neighborhood retail outlets in cities over 100,000 population.[4]

THE STANDARDIZED MEDIUM OF OUTDOOR ADVERTISING

While there are endless ways to deliver sales messages, only a relative handful of *national* media have demonstrated their ability to carry adver-

---

[3] The following data represents an estimate of the economics of transit advertising for 1965:

Number of Displays	200,000	Number of Employees	3,000
Number of Companies	100	Annual Sales Volume	$25,000,000

[4] The following data represents an estimate of the economics for the neighborhood point-of-purchase outdoor advertising for 1965:

Number of Displays	25,000
Number of Companies	200
Number of Employees	500
Annual Sales Volume	$5,000,000

tising messages to given markets economically and efficiently, primarily because each of them, including outdoor, possesses the following important characteristics:

1. Organized.
2. Standardized for ease and economy of use.
3. Packaged to provide market coverage.
4. Measured in terms of delivery.
5. Operated in the public interest.

To the advertiser or his agency, "outdoor advertising" identifies the standard medium of outdoor advertising—one of the several major advertising vehicles for carrying a message to a given market. However, the American public generally uses this same term to designate all outdoor signs. Obviously there is a problem of semantics.

For the purpose of clarification, let us consider previously defined forms of outdoor advertising as being represented by the term "the single

The Single Sign

Picture Credit: Bill Schill, Haddon Heights, N.J.

sign." The single sign, located on a single street, exposes its message to the traffic of that street. This traffic is only a fragment of the total traffic flow in any given urban area, and the over-all urban area is a functional market consisting of the sum total of all population activity. The daily movements of the people residing there and going to work, to shop, to school and to play is the total traffic flow.

While it may be to some degree an oversimplification, the term "medium" implies the exposure of the message to the total market, which, in the case of "outdoor," implies total traffic flow. Consequently, the "outdoor medium" involves a *proper* combination of messages to communicate to the total traffic flow, which is the sum total of all population activity of a market.

THE HISTORY OF THE STANDARDIZED OUTDOOR MEDIUM

The early history of the outdoor advertising medium is in reality the history of mass communication. Until the fifteenth century, public posting was the only means, other than a public address, of disseminating information on a wide basis. Then in 1450, Johannes Gutenberg, a German, invented printing from movable type and the dream of duplicated messages became a reality. The whole concept of mass communication changed. Wide commercial application became economically practical, and advertising, in the modern sense, was launched in the form of the handbill.

About 1480, William Caxton introduced the new type of printing to England, and the first poster printed from type in the English language was made. It measured five by seven inches and was posted on church doors to advertise a religious law book, *The Pyes of Salisbury Use*.

The printing press made possible the development of two media where only one had existed before. The handbill, because it could be distributed in quantity, became a "circulating" medium as contrasted with the "posted" bill. The circulated bill was the progenitor of our newspapers and magazines, while the posted bill was the forerunner of the modern medium of outdoor advertising.

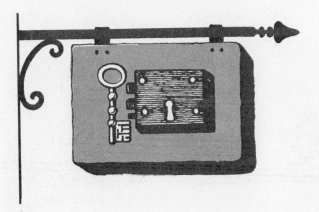

Typical Sign Board in London—17th Century

During the seventeenth and eighteenth centuries, another form of outdoor advertising appeared which was to have a direct effect on bill posting. This was the outdoor sign. As one historian described it: "London was literally darkened with great swinging sign boards of every description during this period." Some of these were outstanding works of art and provided a livelihood for many famous artists. Taverns, bootmakers and apothecaries identified their places of business with signs, symbolic of both trade and firm.

When Alois Senefelder, a German inventor, perfected the lithographic process in 1796, he provided the means for merging these rapidly developing art forms with the all-type handbill, and the illustrated poster became a reality.

Bill-posting methods were rather primitive at this stage of outdoor advertising's development. A boy was given a fistful of bills to stick on the walls and fences of London and paid a few pennies. As the medium became more popular, and good locations scarce, the piecework bill-poster had no scruples about following his competitor around and slapping bills on top of those newly applied.

Gradually, measures were taken to insure exposure of a message for a fixed period of time. This required exclusive permission to post on a given fence or wall. Having purchased this permission, this bill-poster then sought to retain his right by painting his name on the posting area. In order to offer more desirable locations where traffic was heavy, bill-posters began to erect their own structures. Because of the prevalence of the fence as a posting surface, these new structures became known as "fences," a term which persisted for many years.

The posting technique spread rapidly to the colonies, where it was utilized with enthusiasm. The special structure which gradually evolved for use by the bill-poster in giving a listed and protected service for bills was called a "billboard" or merely a "board." The British equivalent is to this day "Hoarding," deriving its name from the hoarding of space on the rough board enclosure surrounding construction work which was commonly used for posting. "Billboard" embedded itself so firmly in the vernacular of the trade and Americana that it has been hard to replace, even though the steel-sectioned poster panels of today bear no resemblance to the "fence."

The early poster advertising in the United States was started spontaneously. Notices of sale of farm stock and equipment, county and

"Hoardings" in England—Early 20th Century

state fairs, theatricals, circuses, horse races, Fourth of July celebrations, carnivals, and medicine shows constituted the early patrons of the industry. Circuses were the most active and the most extensive users of posters in the early days of the medium. Barnum, in this field as in many others, is credited with being one of the pioneers.

Early Example of Posting, Showing the Influence
of Theater Advertising

Even though outdoor advertising in the United States had developed without plan or purpose, it was so effective that by the close of the War Between the States, there were 275 bill-posting·firms employing from two to twenty men each.

Until the beginning of the present century, the manager of the local theater frequently had charge of the outdoor advertising in his city. That came about in a perfectly natural way, as a large part of the posting was for the theater. The manager was well supplied in advance with posters for future shows. If there was no one else available to do the posting, the local manager of the theater would arrange to have it done. The active season for the theater was thirty-two weeks—roughly from the middle of September to the following May—and during this season there was much posting for the theater. During the other twenty weeks, the business was built up for other advertisers who had posting to do. This should not be interpreted to mean that these city plants were wholly taken over during the fall and winter months by the theaters, but during that time they were the principal customers. Consequently, during the summer local advertisers who had posting to do were encouraged to place advertising, and they constituted the poster plant's principal business.

With the strictly commercial posting, employed mainly by food products, patent medicines, soap, cleansing compounds and the like, it was a common practice to secure protection for the position by giving the landlord or tenant trinkets or tickets of admission to a circus. These were freely, if not lavishly, conferred. Subscriptions to magazines, kitchen- and pocket-knives, watches and even jewelry, were used in payment for posting.

In its initial stage, outdoor advertising passed through successive phases of progress which are incident to the development of all industrial undertakings. During this early period, outdoor advertising lacked the

In This Cluster of Billboards from the Twenties, There Are Two Products That Are Still on the Market, Ronald Coleman "In Sound," a Request for Charitable Donations, and a Reminder That "It Pays To Pay Attention To Advertising"

30   PHILLIP TOCKER

benefits of organization, but the potential advertising value of outdoor publicity was clearly demonstrated.

There are many reasons why the year 1870 may be considered the dividing line between ancient and modern outdoor advertising. The perfection of a web-fed printing press, of stereotyping, of paper-folding machines, and of a new lithograph halftone had provided improved mechanical equipment that gave printing and lithography a new field.

Jules Cheret, the first real poster artist, was just coming into his stride in France, and his influence was quickly felt throughout Europe and ultimately reached America. Barnum organized his circus and soon became the most extensive user of outdoor advertising in America, if not the world. It was in 1867 that the earliest recorded leasings of boards occurred in the United States. The firm of Bradbury and Houghteling was formed to give a countrywide paint service, the first of its kind. Previously there had been some 250 firms which offered a limited paint service. Their "services" overlapped, as did those of the early bill-posters, even to the extent of painting over signs recently placed by a competitor.

A little later, in 1872, the firm of Kissam and Allen was formed with the idea of owning and erecting their own poster panels. It was also in this year that the International Bill Posters' Association of North America was formed in St. Louis. This organization continued to function for twelve years, after which it was allowed to lapse. But a new and larger association, under the awkward name of Associated Bill Posters' Association of United States and Canada, was organized in 1891.

It was also during this period that the first of the state bill-posters' associations was formed. Michigan led off in 1875, followed by Indiana, New York, Minnesota, Ohio and Wisconsin, all of which had active associations by 1891.

At the time of the entrance of the theaters into poster advertising, there were improvements in lithographic process for reproducing pictures. The theater posters were limited in size to sheets about 28 by 42 inches. The legitimate use of posters for reputable theaters soon spread to the burlesque shows where such lurid portrayals began to appear that they gave public offense, and the bill-posters, through state and national association action, refused to handle offensive "paper." *This was the earliest recorded censorship exercised by an advertising medium over copy.*

After the permanent organization was launched, developments in the field of outdoor advertising came rapidly. It was in 1891, only twenty-one years after the first announcement of a nationwide paint service by Bradbury and Houghteling, that a meeting of the most enterprising men engaged in the industry was arranged, and a national association of poster men formed. It was called the Associated Bill Posters' Association. This association has functioned continuously and has never ceased to be a live and driving influence. *So far as records reveal, this also was the first national association of advertising men.* The purpose of calling the convention, at which the first national association was formed, was to establish standards and adopt uniform practice as far as possible.

Meanwhile, in 1909, the interests owning the painted bulletins had met and organized, with the purpose similar to those of the poster plant owners. Both organizations early adopted resolutions binding their members to the observance of rules of display which would avoid arousing the animosity of reasonable-minded people. The day of indiscriminate—"as-chance-may-offer"—posting was over, insofar as the members of the association were concerned. Before the policy of leasing had been inaugurated, no assurance was asked or given as to the time the display was to be exhibited. The contracts merely called for

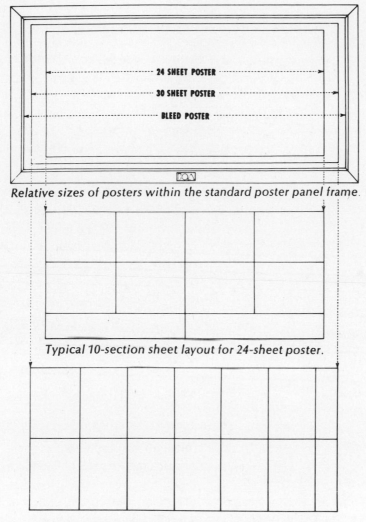

Relative sizes of posters within the standard poster panel frame.

Typical 10-section sheet layout for 24-sheet poster.

Typical 14-section sheet layout for 30-sheet poster.

"posting." With the leasing of space the term "listed and protected showings" was adopted. This meant that each poster was listed as to location and recorded. No other poster could be assigned to that position during the term of the contract. At that time, the contracts scheduled posters for one week, two weeks, etc. The monthly service was unknown. Both associations soon adopted the compulsory plan of using only display space which they controlled, that is, bulletins by the paint interests and poster panels by the poster plants on owned or leased ground.

In 1910, the association began to prescribe the number of locations necessary to give the advertiser coverage in the cities and towns in which his paper was displayed. The introduction of the principle of showings and coverage markedly increased the use of bill-posting as each advertiser received equal treatment.

A definite size for posters was not adopted until the annual meeting of the association in 1912, twenty-one years after the first convention. Not only was the 24-sheet poster made the standard, but its size was determined as 8 feet 8 inches high by 19 feet 6 inches long, the size which now universally prevails (although 8-, 12- and 16-sheets were still in demand). In recognition of this change in the nature of the industry, the name of the association was changed on December 23, 1912, to Poster Advertising Association, Inc. The rating of plants and services was instituted by the association, and a national listing of plants and services was begun.

By 1915, some very definite accomplishments could be noted. The national association was firmly established, with hundreds of members representing several thousand cities and towns. The standard 24-sheet poster had been adopted as the most desirable unit, and the principal feature of the panel structure had been worked out. The frame, design and structural dimensions for the display, the space for white paper blanking and other similar regulations constituting the AA panel had been adopted. (Also by 1915, the painted bulletin owners had formed a national association. In October of 1925, the Poster Advertising Association, Inc., and the Painted Outdoor Advertising Association were merged into the Outdoor Advertising Association of America, Inc.) The outdoor medium had become organized.

Since the turn of the century, a development had occurred which was to broaden the use of outdoor advertising far beyond the wildest dreams of the organizers of the medium. This was the invention and popularity of the automobile, coupled with the gradual development of a network of fine roads. America began to emerge as a nation on wheels, and outdoor was the one means of communicating with this moving market.

On June 15, 1931, a new organization, known as Outdoor Advertising Incorporated, was founded to promote sales for the medium nationally. Outdoor Advertising Incorporated placed at the disposal of advertisers and agencies all the facilities needed to develop a wider and more profitable use of outdoor advertising.

In recognition of the need for continuing research to insure circulation and coverage, the Association of National Advertisers, Inc., requested the cooperation of the Outdoor Advertising Association of America, Inc., and the American Association of Advertising Agencies, Inc., in sponsoring a research project at Harvard University which looked toward the establishment of a more scientific method for determining the circulation-evaluation of outdoor advertising. In 1933, the three associations established the Traffic Audit Bureau, Inc., which has since provided to advertisers authenticated outdoor advertising circulation data which aid in the planning of advertising strategies.

Several conclusions can be drawn from this brief history of outdoor advertising:

1. It is the oldest form of mass communication known to man.
2. It was the earliest recorded censorship exercised by an advertising medium over copy.
3. So far as records reveal, it formed the first national association of advertising men.
4. Its use has grown, largely due to the automobile.

THE MEDIUM TODAY

Today, the standard medium of outdoor advertising is a highly organized, well-regulated business, uniformly available in over 11,000 markets throughout the United States. There are approximately 600 operators of standard outdoor advertising facilities, of which more than 80 percent are members of the national trade association, the Outdoor Advertising Association of America, Inc.

The standardized outdoor advertising medium represents an invested capital of a half-billion dollars in poster panels, painted display bulletins, electric spectaculars, equipment, buildings and real estate.

Approximately 250,000 property owners receive income for rent of space occupied by the standard structures comprising the medium. About 11,000 persons are employed in the operation of organized outdoor advertising plants, including carpenters, steelworkers, tinsmiths, electricians, roofers, painters, poster hangers, laborers, and the necessary foremen, superintendents, clerks and managers. This does not include those commercial artists and lithographic industry employees which are largely dependent upon the outdoor medium. The lithographic industry

*With Automobiles and Roads, the Billboards Moved to
the Small Towns and Countryside*

A Modern Example of a Spectacular

represents an investment of over a quarter-billion dollars and employs thousands of men and women in the production of posters. In addition to this industrial employment, the medium directly and indirectly employs thousands of advertising agency executives, creative artists and sales and promotional personnel.

All levels of government recognize the outdoor medium as a proper and legitimate business activity within the business and commercial areas of the country. Its standardized structures are business structures, like the stores and industries that flank them. They are owned and maintained by the outdoor advertising companies—known as "plants" —and are built on private land which the plants either own or lease. In turn, the plants sell advertising space on the structures to advertisers for a specified period of time.

Standardized outdoor advertising poster panels throughout the country are approximately 12 feet high and 25 feet long, with a uniform copy area of 10 feet 5 inches by 22 feet 8 inches. This standardization enables advertisers to print posters in quantity, with the assurance that they will be displayed uniformly on the structures of any plant in any area. About three million 24- and 30-sheet posters are produced annually in the United States.

Painted bulletins, discussed in detail later, also follow these standards of size and proportion.

All standardized structures conform to rigid engineering standards of safety and construction and local building codes and other ordinances. Illumination specifications similarly conform to the National Electrical Code and local ordinances. Where practical, locations are landscaped to provide an attractive setting for the advertiser's message and for the community.

The terms "24-sheet" and "30-sheet" do not mean that the posters are made up of that many individual pieces of paper, although they were many years ago. Today presses are larger and posters are usually printed in ten to fourteen sections. They are mounted on the outdoor panels, centered within the uniform copy area, and surounded by white blanking paper.

The 24-sheet poster measures 8 feet 8 inches by 19 feet 6 inches. The 30-sheet poster measures 9 feet 7 inches by 21 feet 7 inches, and affords the advertiser 25 percent more display area. A recent development is the "bleed" poster, which extends the artwork right to the frame of the panel by printing on the blanking paper as well as the poster. The size of the bleed poster averages 40 percent larger than the 24-sheet poster. There is no additional space charge for the larger sizes.

In most cities or towns there are one or more outdoor advertising plant operators. Advertisers can buy outdoor advertising nationally, regionally or in any individual local market. The unit of sale in outdoor is the "showing." Showings are available in different intensities just as in other media. For example, in broadcast an advertiser can buy an hour, a minute, or only twenty seconds; in print he can buy multiple pages or fractions of a page. In outdoor, the intensity of a showing is expressed in relative numbers. For example, a #100 showing, a #200 showing, a #50 showing, etc. An outdoor showing is normally sold for a period of thirty days. Showings are normally made up of both regular (non-illuminated) and illuminated panels. Cities with heavy after-dark traffic have a higher ratio of illuminated panels in a showing.

Actual counts of traffic in markets of all sizes by government and private agencies have proved that 10 to 20 percent of the roads carry 80 to 90 percent of the traffic. These are the principal streets leading into the business areas, and it is along the commercial and industrial segments of these streets that poster panels are located. A market is divided into

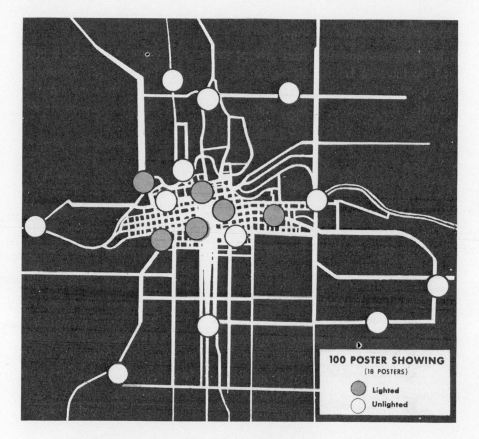

Typical No. 100 Showing, Indicating Panel Distribution

A Painted Bulletin

42   PHILLIP TOCKER

poster zones made up of approximately equal sections of the main traffic arteries used for commerce and industry. The number of poster zones in a market determines the number of panels in a showing. Each #50 showing normally contains one panel in each poster zone; each #100 showing, two panels per zone, etc. This ensures distribution of coverage throughout the market, as well as equality of treatment to all advertisers.

Many plants offer specialized showings to meet the particular needs of individual advertisers. Supermarket showings, for example, offer locations adjacent to or on routes leading to stores of this type. Showings can also be tailored to drugstores, auto dealers, etc. Similarly, they can be set up to concentrate on particular ethnic or demographic groups, or to meet other specialized marketing needs.

The painted bulletins represent less than 10 percent of all standardized outdoor structures, although they account for about 30 percent of outdoor billing. Their greater cost is due to their dominant size and maximum-traffic locations. Due to the distance at which some bulletins are viewed, as in the case of roof locations, the units have to be large enough to be read by the stream of traffic. Sizes customarily range up to 1200 square feet or more. All are customarily illuminated and repainted several times during the year to maintain a fresh, new look.

For dramatic effect, painted bulletins are frequently embellished with cut-out letters and dimensional effects. They extend beyond the frame, but are limited by OAAA standards to a maximum of 5 feet 6 inches at the top and 2 feet at either side. In one popular variation, known as "Tri-vision" or "Multi-Vision," a portion of the face of the board is made up of verticle triangles which turn at intervals, showing three different messages on the same panel. New techniques, such as plastic-faced, back-lighted units, moving messages, unusual treatments of light and color, and similar innovations are constantly being developed and tested.

Bulletins differ from posters in a number of respects in addition to size. The message is hand-painted directly on the face of the bulletin, often in sections in the plant's paint shop. Reproduction by pictorial artists in outdoor plants is faithful to the original art. The sections are then assembled on the site. Bulletins provide coverage by means of size and eye-catching appearance and by location at key spots of high circulation.

They are generally sold for periods of a year or more, not in showings but on the basis of individual locations. The locations can be fixed or rotating. On a rotating or rotary plan, the entire design is transferred from structure to structure at specified intervals. For example, a three-leg rotary plan would provide four months of display at each of three sites during the year. This helps amortize the cost and extend the coverage of an elaborate display.

The outdoor medium is unique in that its audience comes to it in the course of daily traveling about the market. This characteristic is inextricably linked with our mobile society, in which 83 percent of our population live in households owning one or more cars. It accounts for the wide reach (number of people) and high frequency (number of exposures per person) of this medium.

Nielsen, in a study of Los Angeles, found that a #100 showing has a reach of 92 percent and a frequency of twenty-nine times in one month among adults. Studies in Seattle, San Francisco and New York showed consistently similar results. Outdoor advertising, it was also shown, develops its high reach rapidly, with the frequency increasing steadily throughout the month. This combination of reach and frequency results in the high response by the public which outdoor advertising develops for the advertised messages. While it covers the broad spectrum of the population, it delivers its highest levels of frequency of exposure among the upper socio-economic groups—people driving to work in and around the urban area—who constitute the best prospects for the many products and services advertised.

While the outdoor medium by itself delivers substantial coverage of the best prospect group for many advertisers, it is often utilized in a "mix," because all media do not reach all market segments or prospects to the same degree. As such, outdoor complements other media. For example, because those people greatly exposed to the outdoor medium are the lightest watchers of television, outdoor advertising complements TV coverage among them and reinforces TV coverage among the heavy watchers.

A medium that is nationally available to advertisers and one that is standardized, must have an extensive organization. The Outdoor Advertising Association of America, Inc., is the trade association of the standardized outdoor medium, whose plant members operate more than 90 percent of the medium's facilities in this country. The association advises and assists the members of the industry in matters pertaining to public, press and governmental relations. It recommends standards for the construction, illumination and placement of panel and for acceptability of copy.

The Institute of Outdoor Advertising, a new organization, is supported by members of the OAAA, whose purpose is the development of research, creative ideas, promotion and effective uses of the medium. It is a central source of information on outdoor for advertisers, agencies, member plants, sales organizations and the public. The Institute publishes the *Outdoor Buyers Guide,* a quarterly publication containing rates and panels per showing in over 11,000 markets, and the quarterly reports of outdoor advertising expenditures. It sponsors the annual outdoor advertising art competitions and maintains liaison with agencies and advertisers on creative and research aspects of the medium.

Two other organizations serve advertisers and advertising agencies. The National Outdoor Advertising Bureau, Inc., is a service organization cooperatively owned by over 200 advertising agencies and their branches. It gathers cost data and prepares estimates for any combination of markets; does the contracting, billing and paying of individual outdoor plants; performs field inspections; sends posting and paint instructions to all plants on a schedule, and, in short, performs all except the creative functions of an advertising agency in connection with outdoor advertising. The Traffic Audit Bureau, Inc., is a tripartite corporation, sponsored jointly by advertisers, agencies and the outdoor industry. By actual counts of traffic, it audits circulations of outdoor panels. It also evaluates their visibility based on factors such as length of approach, speed of travel, angle of the panel and the relation of the panel to adjacent panels. The combination of circulation and visibility determines the effectiveness of a panel or a complete showing.

IN THE PUBLIC INTEREST

Like all other media, the standardized medium of outdoor advertising has had its problems, but it has survived these to become a major, useful, potent standardized selling force, primarily due to its achievements in the public interest and self-regulation.

However, this long road of evolution has been arduous and beset by formidable and perplexing problems. One of the most frustrating is finding a legal solution to the matter of control and enforcement to prevent abuse of outdoor advertising. For example outdoor advertising is merely a tenant of the right to communicate and the right to private property. These rights belong to others, respectively, the "advertiser" and the "landlord." Notwithstanding the high purpose of providing a legal basis to prevent abuse, there are serious implications in the "tenant" abridging the basic rights of others—"his customers" and "his landlord."

*This Is Not Standardized Outdoor Advertising. There Is Not
a Single Standardized Outdoor Advertising Panel
in This Clutter of Signs*

There is the problem of spacing to avoid "nesting" and "clutter" of signs. Let us assume that there is a 500-foot strip of vacant frontage that has been plotted into ten 50-foot lots. Further, each of these lots is individually owned and all are zoned for business, and outdoor advertising is a "permitted business use." To most people, a large billboard on each of these consecutive 50-foot frontage lots would be excessive. Yet, by what legal process do you permit one landowner to derive revenue for a lawful purpose and deny that right to any of his neighbors? Another aspect of this allocation problem is to decide which advertiser will be granted the use of the hypothetical 500-foot strip to place his sign. By what legal process do you grant the right to one company and withhold it from another?

Another frustrating aspect of seeking control and enforcement to prevent abuse is the limitation of organizational effort to strictly voluntary endeavor for purposes of compliance. Undue group action and coercion to regulate abuse would violate the anti-trust laws. While the organized forms of outdoor advertising have made substantial progress in self-regulation, the unorganized forms, and particularly the off-premise rural roadside sign, depend entirely on the widely varying personal standards of self-control of individual advertisers and/or sign companies.

The organized and standardized outdoor advertising medium has long recognized that its business must be conducted with due consideration of the public interest. To provide safe structures, building code requirements and accepted engineering practices have been established by the association in cooperation with such groups as American Standards Association, Bureau of Standards and the Building Officials Conference of America. Extensive research has been conducted by the association over many years and at many universities. This is a continuing process and further studies are being made to improve structures and provide a more dynamic means of mass communication.

Industry leaders realize, however, that what imperfections do exist in the standardized medium should be corrected. Through the Outdoor Advertising Association of America, a program has been going on during the past several years to persuade operators to eliminate the minority of substandard structures and step up maintenance practices. Results are evident in the thousands of new Association-Loewy panels being constructed each year, in the addition of modern fluorescent illumination to these structures, in the increase of landscaped locations and in the increased use of cantilevered construction with its clean, modern lines.

For over forty years the Association has maintained a code of ethics defining the recommended placement of outdoor advertising structures and the display of advertising copy in terms of the best public interest.

As owners and operators of standardized Outdoor Advertising displays, we, the members of Outdoor Advertising Association of America, Inc., have voluntarily pledged strict adherence to a rigid code of practices, and endorse adoption of these principles by state and local governments, as follows:

WE share the public interest in natural scenic beauty, parks, and historical monuments. We do not erect our advertising displays in such areas.

WE believe in and support zoning based on sound community planning.

WE locate our structures in urban areas only where business exists or is permitted under zoning.

WE build displays in rural areas along highways only where other business exists or is permitted by state or local regulations.

WE locate our structures with discretion and good taste with respect to frequency and concentration.

WE place outdoor advertising displays only upon property we own or lease for that purpose.

WE observe rigid standards of design, construction and maintenance so that our displays will be attractive.

WE only display outdoor advertising which is truthful in every respect and in accordance with high moral standards.

WE actively and continuously support worthy public causes through our contribution of outdoor advertising displays.

Supplementing its Code of Practices, for many years the Outdoor Advertising Association of America, Inc., has remained sensitive to the public interest and consistently urged its membership to propose measures for reasonable regulation at local and state levels. This activity has taken the positive form of suggested zoning ordinances, generally restricting the erection and maintenance of outdoor advertising structures to commercial and industrial areas—or stated in another way, to prohibit them in residential areas.

More recently, in October of 1960, the association distributed to all members a proposed statewide regulatory act to protect scenic areas and require licensing, permits and bonds in order to provide responsible operation. Again in October, 1964, the association prepared and distributed to its membership for presentation to legislatures a Model Highway Scenic Area Act providing for the establishment of such areas by law and regulating and restricting the placement of all signs therein. This was followed in November, 1964, by another model legislative proposal for over-all regulation, upgrading and strengthening the 1960 model.

An official and publicly acknowledged recognition of the association's activity in this direction was made by the Oregon Scenic Area Board's report (December, 1964).

Historically, the public relations objective of the standardized outdoor medium has been similar to that of other American businesses: to operate in the best interest of its customers and the general public. Yet, it faces special problems in the form of misconceptions held by a vocal minority and repeated by certain segments of the press that sometimes result in discriminatory legislation being enacted.

These misconceptions fall into five general categories: that all advertising outdoors is "outdoor advertising," that "billboards line the highways," that outdoor advertising is a traffic hazard, that outdoor advertising is "ugly," and last, that outdoor advertising is a purely commercial medium, transmitting only commercial messages to the American public.

Taking these points as follows:

A. Only the outdoor advertising medium employs standardized outdoor advertising structures, scientifically located to deliver a message to a specific market. This coverage can be provided on a selective basis to a segment of the market, to an individual market or to a group of markets simultaneously through the United States. Other forms of outdoor advertising, such as directional signs, commercial and identification signs, and name plates, have a place in the economy, but they are not a part of the medium of standardized outdoor advertising and are not intended to provide coverage on a market basis.

B. Standardized outdoor advertising is a basically urban medium; 90 percent of its structures are located in urban areas which are zoned for business or commercial use. Many studies have shown that standardized outdoor advertising represents less than 4 percent of all commercial occupancies along roadways which are considered as having "roadside problems." It is important to note that all these roadside occupancies are legal.

C. There is no evidence whatsoever that outdoor advertising has been a contributing factor to a single traffic accident. An independent study made by the Michigan State Highway Department in cooperation with the U.S. Bureau of Public Roads showed no correlation between roadside accidents and outdoor advertising. Dr. A. R. Lauer, a recognized traffic safety expert, undertook an objective research study in the Driving Laboratory of Iowa State University. His study showed that "numerous signs in the driver's field of vision in no way influenced efficiency at the wheel adversely." If anything, his report concluded, the signs seemed slightly beneficial—by about 10 percent—in that they provided visual stimuli tending to relieve highway monotony and to keep the driver alert.

D. Aesthetics is a much more difficult question to answer since it is a matter of subjective taste. However, these points should be made: Outdoor advertising displays themselves are simple and functional, and outdoor operators try to make them as attractive as they can. More than one-half in use today are of a new type specifically designed for the outdoor medium by Raymond Loewy, noted industrial designer. Outstanding artists design the copy which is displayed on outdoor panels and bulletins.

E. For a number of years, outdoor advertising has had an "editorial concept," embodied in the contributed display of posters and painted bulletins for national and local public service causes. Industry has consistently contributed a portion of its facilities to public service, advancing or contributing to the public health, safety, morals and general welfare. The outdoor advertising medium and its personnel on a continuing basis support many worthwhile national and local causes by donating space and by participating in the campaigns. A sizable collection of awards and commendations testify to the appreciation by governmental, charitable and community organizations and agencies of outdoor's support.

Because outdoor appeals primarily to automotive traffic, the industry's primary year-round campaign is its own traffic safety program. For many years it has joined with state and local safety and highway authorities, law enforcement officials and civic organizations in a cooperative effort to prevent traffic accidents. Contributions in space to this campaign approach a million dollars annually. More than half of the industry's support of national public service programs is given to campaigns conducted through the Advertising Council. This organization, which the outdoor industry helped to found, is private, nonprofit and nonpartisan and is jointly supported and operated by advertisers, agencies and media groups. Recent campaigns included advertising aid to religion, education, the American Red Cross, United Community Drives, U.S. Savings Bonds, and other major U.S. Government projects.

At the local level, outdoor advertising has assisted communities in attracting more industry or more visitors, in beautifying areas, in preventing fires, in gaining support for health, education and religion, in raising money for charities and in working on a multitude of local problems.

THE POSITION OF THE OUTDOOR MEDIUM ON HIGHWAY BEAUTIFICATION

No presentation of the standardized outdoor advertising medium would be complete without reviewing its role and position on highway beautification. Through its trade association, the medium has long recognized that there are areas of scenic beauty upon which no business should encroach. It also recognized that there is a place for legitimate business activity in commercial, industrial and business areas. Consequently, the OAAA, as the spokesman for the medium, has historically and consistently opposed discriminatory legislation that failed to recognize that the outdoor medium is an integral part of the business and marketing function and should enjoy the same rights as other business.

The writer was a participant and panelist at the White House Conference on Natural Beauty held in Washington, D.C., on May 24 and 25, 1965. The following is quoted from the report of the Roadside Control Committee as contained in the report to the President:

> . . . A majority of the panelists were of the opinion that no off-premise advertising should be permitted in any areas adjacent to

the Primary System or Interstate System. One panelist (Mr. Tocker) was of the view that off-premise advertising should be permitted in commercial, industrial, and business areas without regard to their being zoned as such.

A vote was taken at a panel meeting following the panel session, and all panelists present, with one exception, voted to recommend that no off-premise advertising be permitted in any areas adjacent to the Primary System and the Interstate System. Senator Maurine Neuberger and Mr. Bridwell [at the time of the writing of this paper the Federal Highway Administrator] were unable to be present at this meeting. Senator Neuberger requested that the report reflect that she would have voted to exclude off-premise advertising in areas adjacent to the Primary System and the Interstate System, except those zoned for commercial or industrial usage. Mr. Bridwell has asked that the report show that he would have voted to recommend that off-premise advertising be permitted in areas zoned for commercial or industrial uses and in areas where the land use is, in fact, commercial or industrial as defined by appropriate regulation.

In line with the writer's position, the board of directors of the association agreed to support the Highway Beautification Act of 1965 sent to the Congress by the White House.

The resolution of the board supporting the President's bill was conditioned upon fair compensation being provided for lawfully placed structures that would be rendered nonconforming under the law, and Congress so provided. Proceeding even further in the direction of supporting the beautification program, in December, 1965, less than two months after the effective date of the law, the association prepared and disseminated to its members for proposal to their state legislatures a model state law designed to implement the federal law, and it urged its members to seek adoption thereof. This action was carried out in spite of a general reluc-

Example: Public Service—Painted Bulletin

tance on the part of many state officials and substantial segments of the business community.

In summary, the standardized medium of outdoor advertising is particularly equipped and organized to deliver advertising messages to every American who goes out-of-doors.

Its influence reaches the people in every city and town without getting in their way or asking them to expend any effort.

It delivers its message without the requirement of a purchase or payment of any kind on the part of the reader or viewer and imposes no distinction as to occupation, age, sex, or status.

It is an important business tool that creates demand for the products and services of our mass production system.

Its units of display are business structures like the stores and industries that flank them.

As a responsible salesman, it is a well-regulated, lawful and legal business that recognizes and serves in the public interest.

As a good neighbor, it is a persuasive tool in promoting community spirit—providing public service messages throughout the country.

All that it asks in return, as the oldest of the advertising media, is to continue to do business where others do business, under the same freedoms and limitations.

III. HUMAN RESPONSE TO VISUAL ENVIRONMENTS IN URBAN AREAS

Cyril Herrmann

There is a new, national concern for the quality of our environment. This concern is expressed in a desire for beauty, both in conserving the natural environment and finding better ways of planning and improving the man-made environment. Hundreds of millions of dollars are being spent on programs of land acquisition, landscaping, park development, undergrounding of utilities and highway beautification. The objective is to preserve and improve the environment of a rapidly urbanizing America.

It is becoming apparent that measures of effectiveness of these efforts are lacking. When it comes to translating the generalized objective into goals and criteria for the implementation of specific programs, it is discovered we lack accurate and comprehensive information on human response to manmade environments. Such information is essential if we are to evaluate proposals, establish policies, resolve conflicts and make progress in implementing constructive programs.

Recognizing this need, the firm of Arthur D. Little, Inc., developed a research proposal designed to:

1. Identify, define, and evaluate the significant variables which produce perceptions of order and disorder in visual environments;
2. devise a standard system for measuring individual evaluation and response to the visual environment; and
3. test the responses of individuals to alterations of significant variables in certain visual environments.

The aim of the research was to evolve a method of analysis for studying observer evaluation of the existing visual environments.

In a preliminary exploration with a representative of the Bureau of Public Roads, we were encouraged to continue the conversations that had been going on from the time of the inception of the idea with Ross Barrett, President of Foster & Kleiser and a member of the Outdoor Advertising Association of America (OAAA). In view of the impending passage of the Highway Beautification Act, it was determined that there was a valid basis for asking for private support of the research. The OAAA does not have a large research budget at its command but it authorized a research grant of $80,000 to fund the first phase of research. The agreement provided that:

1. Emphasis be given to developing a method of measuring human reaction to the roadside environment. Outdoor advertising was to be treated as one element in the total environment.
2. Any method of measuring human reaction to the roadside environment would be fully published and made available to the research and planning professions and to government agencies.
3. An advisory committee would be selected from the planning community. This was to insure the research design met the needs of the planning community. Everyone agreed there should be no bias whatsoever in favor of billboards.

The Arthur D. Little project team was made up of the following key members: Warren Deem, project director, and Dr. Robert Barringer, Roger Malek, AIA, Professor Philip Thiel and Dr. Gary Winkel.

It has been the objective of the team to continue a dialogue with the planning community during the progress of the work. Most of our effort has been devoted to the research and to the analysis, in considerable depth, of the research subjects participating in the experiment.

The report which follows will demonstrate that this experimental research program has been successful. A method of measuring human response to visual environments in urban areas has been established. This method has validity and reliability. It marks an additional step in bringing scientific method to the analysis of environmental problems where the identification of human response is of critical importance.

I. PROBLEM

A. GENERAL BACKGROUND AND METHOD OF APPROACH

The experimental development of techniques for measuring and analyzing human responses to the environment is a complicated task involving many factors. This complexity required using a variety of research tools and methods. Because of this, the study should be regarded as an experiment in relating objective research to urban design. Basic research in psychology and visual analysis have produced the battery of techniques used in this study. Work in related fields which has been undertaken at the Massachusetts Institute of Technology by Kevin Lynch, at Harvard University by Norman Mackworth and at the University of Illinois by Charles Osgood underlies many elements of this study, as does additional original work by several of the study participants.

This study was limited to a consideration of the urban highway as seen in a sequence of slides. Initially, the study also has been confined to commercial environments in urban areas. A selected group of observers were presented with a controlled series of experiences. At the same time, we measured by a battery of tests the nature of their evaluations and attitudes. The input was a series of slides shown in sequence. The slides were shown for five to ten seconds each, with a similar interval between each slide for calibration.

Landscaped Route As It Is

60   CYRIL HERRMANN

Commercial Route As It Is

In our initial tests, because of technical problems, the slides were in black and white; the first task was to obtain an accurate measure of the eye movements of each observer. This was done by using a Mackworth eye movement camera. As each slide appeared before each observer, a movie record was made of those points in the slide on which his eye fixated.

The second task was to measure the response of the observer to what he was seeing. We used a bipolar adjective scale, similar to Osgood's semantic differential, to measure the direction and intensity of reaction to what was seen. A measurement of creativity and tolerance of ambiguity versus a desire for order and other factors was made using the Barron-Welsh art test. The study also included depth interviews and questionnaires which recorded a considerable amount of data about the characteristics of the observer.

B. EXPERIMENTAL PROCEDURE

The observer was introduced to the task of the experiment, calibrated on the eye movement camera and shown a route (either "commercial," or "landscaped") with no changes, for a baseline measurement.

He was then asked to evaluate the route on the bipolar adjective scale. He was next shown and asked to observe four different sets of slides, from the same route, each with different sets of elements removed from the environment. (These sets of elements are billboards, utility poles, billboards and utility poles, billboards and utility poles and other signs.) After seeing each set, each observer was asked for his judgment concerning the similarity or difference of the route just seen compared with the original route. If the observer noted a difference in the character of the original route, he was asked if he wanted to change his adjective evaluation of the new route, and if so, was asked to do this. Finally, the observer was asked to fill out the demographic questionnaire, the personality questionnaire, take the Barron-Welsh art test and to make a rating of the priority of urban problems.

C. RESULTS OF TEST

The method is effective—that is, for the sample of users (subjects) tested, for the sample of roadside environments (inputs) experienced and for the levels of response studied (i.e., detection and evaluation), we were able to achieve both (1) reliability and (2) validity in the measured responses of these subjects to these inputs.

(1) *"Reliability"* refers to the method's ability to repeat, or predict, a user response, if the attitudinal characteristics of the observer and the characteristics of the input are known.

(2) *"Validity"* refers to the "reality" of those subject responses, or their relevance to the "real world." In other words, the measured evaluative responses of the subjects systematically reflected changes in the environmental inputs.

II. GENERAL FINDINGS

A. PRACTICAL FINDINGS

It was found that response to billboards was not as significantly related to considerations of environmental quality as were some other aspects of the roadside environment. This does not mean that the presence or absence of billboards is not noticed. It simply indicates that, for our sample, in our tests the presence or absence of billboards in the routes used in the experiment is not especially critical in achieving what is called environmental quality. Furthermore, our subjects' response to the effect of billboards in the environment depended on the nature of the environment itself.

The majority of those who were most vociferous about outlawing billboards did not reevaluate the route when the billboards were removed. Only 30 percent of the total group were in favor of legislation which

Landscaped Route Minus Billboards

64   CYRIL HERRMANN

Commercial Route Minus Billboards

would outlaw billboards. The percentage for commercial and landscaped route observers was 27 percent and 32.6 percent, respectively.

For the commercial route, the removal of utility poles, billboards and other signs resulted in an evaluation of the transformed route which was more similar to the evaluations of the route in its original state. When the above three object groups were removed, most of the observers noticed a difference, and some were surprised that they did not like the resulting environment as well as they thought they might.

To the extent that the observers looked at billboards, the route was rated as more simple, whereas the extent to which they looked at utility poles, the effect was more complicated. Billboards are positively correlated with the simplicity-complexity scale whereas the utility poles are negatively correlated.

B. THEORETICAL FINDINGS

It appears that the attitudinal characteristics of the observer are a more important factor in causing his evaluation of the roadside than the demographic characteristics. The only demographic factor that showed some degree of correlation with the bipolar adjective and personality factors was the amount of education of the observer. The greater his education, the more he sees the road as depressing and monotonous, and the more negative his attitudes toward the roadside. (See Table 1.)

We were able to identify a set of attitudes which apparently signified a need for order and predictability, at the expense of diversity or complexity. This factor, Factor 2 of the personality questionnaire, correlates negatively with Barron-Welsh scores. A low Barron-Welsh score indicates a quiet and ordered person who is not high in originality or individuality. The total number of eye fixations correlates negatively with this group, which indicates a focuser. This factor also correlates with older people,

TABLE I
CORRELATION MATRIX

	Age	Income	Rural	Education	BW Total	Bipol I	Bipol II	Bipol III	Pers I	Pers II	Pers III	Total Fix
Age		-.356			(-.437)					.516		
Income			-.433 (.372)		.341		.311		-.374	-.402		
Rural												
Education						(.642)	(-.406)	(.522)	(.332)		(-.342)	
BW Total						(.348)	(-.307)	(.431)		(-.426)	(-.381)	.360
Bipol I							.717 (-.769)	.945 (.914)	.655 (.529)			
Bipol II								-.815 (-.895)	-.670 (-.590)		-.524 (-.546)	
Bipol III									.621 (.573)		.464 (.622)	
Pers I										(-.426)	-.421 (-.566)	-.350
Pers II												
Pers III												-.312
Total Fix												

(.372) Landscape route
-.356 Commercial route

having lived in a rural background during the early years, lower income, not taking art courses and recognition of the route shown on the slides.

We were able to identify three consistent groups of adjectives used in evaluating the roadside environment. The first group was descriptive of an emotional-aesthetic reaction to the roadside as monotonous and depressing. The second factor was descriptive of the physical characteristics of the roadside, such as simplicity and complexity, etc. The third factor was concerned with the utility of the roadside in terms of its usefulness or effectiveness.

There was a useful correlation between the simple numerical descriptors used to quantify the physical stimulus and the observers ratings of simplicity and complexity. Bipolar Factor I (the emotional aesthetic factor) was not strongly correlated with the numerical descriptors, whereas Bipolar Factor II (the factor descriptive of physical characteristics) was much more closely correlated with these descriptors.

The method used for describing the physical stimulus was a simple numercial indicator which was based on counting the number of elements and computing the relative area of the objects within each descriptive category (i.e., utility poles, billboards, other signs, etc.), as well as counting the number of overlaps between objects. The numerical indicators were arrived at by taking the product number of elements, difference between areas, and number of overlaps in various combinations. A selective regression analysis was made between eye movement data, bipolar adjective factors, the above products and the separate items (i.e., number of elements, overlaps, etc.) to determine which correlations were the most significant.

C. SELECTED DETAILED FINDINGS

1. Attitudes of Sample to the Priority of Urban Problems

It was our feeling that we cannot deal with the problem of billboards, or any other problem presumably affecting the quality of environment, without considering it in the context of other urban problems. In a survey of the literature to identify what are currently thought to be the major problems affecting the quality of the environment, they were found to be litter, air pollution, traffic congestion, junkyards, billboards, noise, overpopulation, poor design, lack of planning, destruction of nature, dilapidated buildings, overhead wires, dust and dirt. In our questionnaire we asked our observers to rank these problems in order of priority of attack The data generally suggests, contrary to our expectations, that our observers do not agree at all between or among themselves about the order of importance of these problems. This would suggest that it would be impossible to develop a priority system which would match the expectations of the individuals who are presumably affected.

2. Personality Types

Each subject was rated on a scale for all three personality factors. One who scores high on Personality Factor I may score low or high on Factors II or III. Therefore, the personality factors are not to be thought of as single individuals, but as dominant characteristics which each observer has to a greater or lesser degree.

The results of a factor analysis of the personality questionnaires has revealed three apparently basic orientations to the man-made environment. Personality Factor I can be characterized as a pessimism toward the roadside and the businessman's involvement in it. Personality Factor II reflects a deeper concern with the problem of the environmental complexity and the dampening of the diversity of stimulation, and its opposite: the need for order and predictability. Personality Factor III is characterized by an "action" orientation and a desire for excitement. This group felt that most billboards help to make a trip more interesting.

The observers who score high on personality Factor I tend to rate the original routes as "depressing," "monotonous," and "dull"; and they tend to rate the urban highway as "cluttered," "complex," and "disorganized" as well as "inefficient" and "useless."

The observers who score high on personality Factor III tend to see the roadside as "exciting" and "lively," "complex," "cluttered," "disorganized," "useful," "efficient" and "necessary."

3. Evaluations of the Routes

Noticing a "change in the route" during the experiment is defined as noticing a difference in the over-all character. In all cases, the change was with reference to the original baseline route; the unchanged route was shown first.

A factor analysis of the results of the bipolar adjective evaluations revealed three primary groupings which we have identified as Factors I, II and III.

Factor I can be characterized as a monotony-variety scale. The adjective pairs grouped in this factor include: impersonal-personal; monotonous-varied; dull-exciting; tiresome-refreshing.

Factor II can be characterized as a simplicity-complexity scale. The adjective pairs grouped in this factor include: simple-complex; harmonious-discordant; balanced-unbalanced.

Factor III can be characterized as a uselessness-usefulness scale. The adjective pairs grouped in this factor include: useless-effective; and ineffective-effective.

Each observer's bipolar adjective evalautions were given a score on bipolar Factors I, II and III. These scores were compared to a completely neutral (i.e., indifferent) score on the bipolar scale which we have called that of Mr. Bland, who, of course, is fictitious.

As the object categories were removed from the environment, the subject's reevaluations were expressed as a change in score with respect to Mr. Bland. These changes were then subtracted from the initial evaluation scores to give a score expressing the new evaluation of the route. These scores were further described by positive and negative directions.

4. The Results of the Observer Evaluations

Seventy-eight percent of the observers noticed a difference as objects were removed from the highway sequences. (See Table 2.) This would indicate that people were involved in the experiment and were looking for differences. If the observers had not been instructed to look for changes in the displays, the percentages might have decreased. In a sense, by following this procedure we were biasing the observers to notice the difference.

When billboards were removed, few people noticed a difference in the over-all environment, in both the landscaped and commercial routes. Only 32.4 percent of the observers noticed a difference in the commercial route and 37.2 percent noticed a difference in the landscaped route.

Most of the observers who did notice a difference when billboards were removed did not change their evaluation of the route. That is, they felt it was no better or no worse than the original route. For the commercial route, only 8.1 percent of those who noticed a difference reevaluated. For the landscaped route, 11.6 percent of those who noticed a difference reevaluated. More people who noticed a difference reevaluated the landscaped route rather than the commercial route.

TABLE II
SUMMARY OF OBSERVERS WHO NOTICED A DIFFERENCE AND COMMENTS DURING TEST INTERVIEWS

	Route	Percent who noticed a difference	Of those who noticed a difference, percent who reevaluated	Interviews During Test — Positive Comments					Negative Comments				
				UP	BB	OS	Bldg.	Lnd.	UP	BB	OS	Bldg.	Lnd.
COMMERCIAL	Billboards	32.4	8.1	1					1				
	Utility Poles	59.5	16.2							8		1	
	UP + BB	64.9	2.7							2		1	
	UP + BB + OS	83.8	40.5			2			1				
LANDSCAPED	Billboards	37.2	11.6	1					3	4	1	1	
	Utility Poles	53.5	11.6							3	4	3	
	UP + BB	67.4	34.9									2	
	UP + BB + OS	83.7	23.3	1					1				1

The commercial route initially was evaluated by all reevaluators as more monotonous and depressing, and less simple and harmonious than the landscaped route. When the billboards were removed from the commercial route, it was rated less monotonous and depressing, and more simple and harmonious. The same was true for the landscaped route except that the shift was not as great. The monotony score for the commercial route shifted from 14.39 to 6.97, the simplicity score from 1.06 to 14.86, whereas for the landscaped route the monotony score shifted from 9.84 to –3.12 and the simplicity score from 4.6 to 1.94. (See Table 3.)

When utility poles were removed from the commercial route, the route became much more varied, exciting and lively, and much more simple. The score when utility poles were removed from the commercial route

TABLE III

BIPOLAR ADJECTIVE FACTOR SCORES

Route	Commercial		Landscaped	
	Factor I Monotony	Factor II Simplicity	Factor I Monotony	Factor II Simplicity
Route as is (all initial evaluations)	14.39	1.06	9.84	4.60
Minus Billboards	– 6.97	14.86	– 3.12	1.94
Minus Utility Poles	–33.55	26.72	—	—
Minus BB and UP	—	—	–31.89	25.59
Minus BB, UP and other signs	– 0.78	7.09	–21.24	27.34

was −33.55 whereas for billboards it was only −6.97. When the utility poles were removed from the route the reevaluators' eye fixations on billboards increased 1.0 percent on the commercial route and 3.3 percent on the landscaped route.

Generally speaking, as utility poles and billboards, separately or both, where removed from the routes the observers rated these routes as progressively less monotonous and more simple. However, when utility poles, billboards and other signs were removed from the commercial route, a shift in the direction of their evaluations toward the initial evaluations took place.

TABLE IV

CHANGE IN PERCENTAGE OF TOTAL EYE FIXATIONS

	Buildings		Trees		Sky		Land	
	Com-mer-cial	Land-scaped	Com-mer-cial	Land-scaped	Com-mer-cial	Land-scaped	Com-mer-cial	Land-scaped
Route as is (original %)	15.7	5.0	1.3	20.2	22.4	17.5	14.7	19.7
Minus Billboards	− 0.2	0.0	0.5	8.2	9.4	− 0.5	−13.0	− 4.5
Minus Utility Poles	8.5	—	0.4	4.5	11.9	—	− 4.7	—
Minus UP & BB	—	4.4	—	9.0	—	15.4	—	− 4.4
Minus UP, BB & other signs	19.2	4.0	2.4	8.1	8.5	11.1	0.3	2.9

The eye fixations indicated that in the commercial route a progressive removal of elements results in a greater increase in eye fixations on the buildings. Whereas on the landscaped route, when utility poles, billboards and other signs were removed, a greater increase in eye fixations on trees resulted. (See Table 4.)

This shift in evaluation is probaly not only a function of attention to trees in the landscaped route or the buildings in the commercial route but also a realization that the signs (both other and billboards) have been removed. On the basis of the interviews it probably would be safe to say that the removal of on-premise signs was the single most important factor in producing a reevaluation. A few observers remarked spontaneously that they were surprised to find that the removal of utility poles, billboards and other signs actually produced a less satisfying effect than they expected.

III. DESCRIPTION OF THE EXPERIMENT

A. CHARACTERISTICS OF THE SAMPLE

The sample of subjects to be tested was obtained by placing advertisements in the *Seattle Times* and in the student newspaper of the University of Washington. Subjects were selected to provide a broad demographic range. The subjects were each paid $7.50 for participation in the experiment. The sample was composed of two groups; a student group and a non-student group. Each group numbered forty observers, a total of eighty.

The majority of the non-student sample fell in the age range of from twenty to twenty-five years of age. One portion of the sample was raised primarily in small towns, of from twenty to fifty thousand population;

Landscaped Route Minus Utility Poles

76   CYRIL HERRMANN

Commercial Route Minus Utility Poles

the other portion in large cities of from 500 thousand to one million. Their preferred place of residence followed very much the size of city in which they spent their early years, although most of the sample presently lived in a large city. The income level of the non-students was mainly in the $5,000 to $10,000 per year group. The majority of the sample had completed high school and some college but did not necessarily complete college. The majority of the non-students had very few classes in aesthetics, art history or drawing. They represented a wide variety of occupations.

The majority of the students fell in the age range of from eighteen to twenty-two years. Most of them were raised in chiefly urban environments: cities of 200,000 to 1,000,000. Their preferred place of residence was similar to their actual place of residence, i.e., urban. Most of them expected to live in urban areas. As might be expected, the family income of the student sample was generally higher than the non-student sample, the median being about $10,000 per year. The students did not have a great deal of training in aesthetics, art history, or art practice, but did represent a wide variety of majors.

B. EXPERIMENTAL PROCEDURE

The observer was introduced to the task of the experiment, calibrated on the eye movement camera and shown a route (either the "commercial" route or the "landscape" route) with no changes, for a baseline measurement. He was then asked to evaluate the route on the bipolar adjective scale. He was next shown and asked to observe four different sets of slides, from the same route, each with different sets of elements removed from the environment. (These sets of elements are billboards, utility poles, billboards and utility poles, billboards and utility poles and other signs.) After seeing each set, the observer was asked for his judgment concerning the similarity or difference of the route just seen compared with the original route. If the observer noted a difference he was asked if he wanted to change his adjective evaluation of the new route and, if so, was asked to do this. Finally, the observer was asked to fill out the demographic questionnaire, the personality questionnaire, and to make a rating of the priority of urban problems.

IV. ANALYTICAL TECHNIQUES BIPOLAR ADJECTIVES

A. FACTOR ANALYSIS

The results of a single evaluation or reevaluation of the sequences shown are represented by a series of sixty-four numbers, the ratings on each of sixty-four bipolar adjectives scales. Since there were eighty initial evaluations and fifty-four reevaluations, it was clearly impossible to analyze these results directly.

Furthermore, many pairs were closely synonymous with other pairs and thus were, at least partially, redundant. For instance, the pair "monotonous-varied" and "dull-exciting" are closely related in concept. In fact, they were found to be closely related in their usage; that is, if a subject rated a route fairly monotonous, he almost always rated that route fairly dull as well. Similarly, a route rated "varied" was usually rated "exciting."

A statistical method called "factor analysis" was used for the analysis. In this method, groups of adjective pairs with high correlation are sought and identified. These are arranged into clusters of closely related adjective pairs, called "factors." Three factors were prominent enough to have statistical significance, the remaining clusters were closely correlated among themselves.

With the three adjective clusters identified, it was possible to use a weighted average of adjective pairs to compute a factor score. For example:

Landscaped Route Minus Billboards and Utility Poles

80   CYRIL HERRMANN

Commercial Route Minus Billboards and Utility Poles

		Factor I	Factor II
Subject 39	Evaluation (Route 0)	14.3	26.7
Subject 39	Reevaluation (Route 4)	28.3	39.1
Subject 27	Evaluation (Route 0)	18.0	20.9

These scores indicated that Subject 39 considered Route 4 (with utility poles and all signs removed) more monotonous (Factor 1) and more simple. Subject 27 rated the original route a little more monotonous than did Subject 39, but less simple.

Scores for Factor I were computed for each evaluation. Average scores for the initial evaluation were computed for the commercial and landscaped routes separately, and for the student and non-student observers separately.

For all observers who reevaluate, the mean difference was computed for each factor, between the reevaluation score and the original route.

B. PERSONALITY FACTORS

In order to characterize the observers in their attitudes toward the urban scene and toward highway visual factors, each observer was asked to fill out a questionnaire consisting of ninety-seven questions. The same techniques of factor analysis were applied to the questionnaire answers.

C. EYE FIXATIONS AND ROUTE DESCRIPTORS

The eye fixation data, route descriptors and Factors I and II from the bipolar scales were analyzed together using a multiple regression technique. An equation was set up with the following format:

$$F = a + b.x$$

where F represents the Factor 1 score or the Factor 2 score and x is an individual eye fixation factor, or a route descriptor. The constants, a and b, are computed to fit the data for the five routes as closely as possible. Of course, the equation does not generally represent an exact fit to the data. Each route will have a residual score representing the lack of fit to that route. These residuals are then examined for significant correlations with other factors.

One interesting finding was that the route descriptors used to characterize the physical stimulus were more strongly correlated with Factor II (simplicity) than with Factor I (monotony). Furthermore, when an equation had been set up with Factor II:

$$\left. \begin{array}{l} \text{Factor II} \\ \text{Landscaped Route} \end{array} \right) = a + b \cdot (\text{a descriptor})$$

then utility poles and overlaps were negatively correlated with the residuals. In other words:

1. The more attention given to utility poles (the less attention given to other factors), the more complex the route appeared.
2. The more attention given to overlaps of elements (the less attention given to other factors), the more complex the route appeared.

V. FURTHER RESEARCH

A. TECHNICAL COMMUNICATION WITH PROFESSIONAL GROUPS

We recommend that the OAAA make a modest research grant of $25,-000 to permit us to develop a report which includes some of the actual photographic materials used in the research. We would present this report to appropriate professional groups and governmental agencies. This should assist materially in obtaining a further research grant to carry on the research which was initiated by the OAAA. If there were

Landscaped Route Minus Billboards,
Utility Poles and Other Signs

84   CYRIL HERRMANN

Commercial Route Minus Billboards,
Utility Poles and Other Signs

any funds available beyond the communications tasks, we would undertake further analysis and data cuts of the information gathered in the present research.

B. FUTURE RESEARCH

The directions of future research, refinement of present methodology and the application of the present research to more focused practical problems are parallel investigations.

Using the same methodology, as the research focuses on various specific problems the content of the bipolar adjective and the personality questionnaire will accordingly be refined and standardized where appropriate. Fundamental questions posed by the findings of the present research, which are important to investigate further, include:

1. To what extent is aesthetic evaluation of the roadside related to safety?
2. What are some of the behavioral and attitudinal correlates of those making up Personality Factors I, II and III?
3. How do different kinds of environments affect Personality Types I, II and III?
4. What are some of the factors affecting public education about the environment and its problems?
5. In view of the controversy about the Hess technique, is it possible to develop more sensitive physiological measurements of human response to the environment, or to make further investigations as to its applicability for this kind of research?
6. We must do further research to determine the relationships which might exist between attitude and behavior, under alternative payoff structures. Cost-benefit studies related to the perception of environmental alternatives.

7. What are the variables involved in rating the roadside environment on Factor I of the bipolar adjectives (evaluative)? Once having identified these variables, are they capable of change?
8. One of the areas not included in this study involves the consideration of various aspects of the roadside environment under different contexts. For example, in the present study evaluative responses of the highway apparently are related to attitudes about business and the roadside; however, we must learn how attitudes about the roadside will change as a function of what it is a corridor to or from. For instance, if the observer were told that he was taking the commercial route into the city to go to work, its design qualities might be seen differently than if he were using it to leave the city to go to a resort for a vacation.
9. Problems of location, spacing, size and design of the objects in the environment as they relate to observer attitudes and evaluations can be approached utilizing the methodology of the present research. It will be possible to establish thresholds of evaluation for observers with different attitudinal characteristics.

IV. THE USE OF EMINENT DOMAIN AND POLICE POWER TO ACCOMPLISH AESTHETIC GOALS

Michael Litka

Regulation of outdoor advertising raises the problem of accommodating the interest of the community with the landowner's traditional interest in a rather unrestricted use of his land. A particularly perplexing aspect in this accommodation of interests is the drafting of regulatory legislation based upon the aesthetic considerations of the community. No one can deny the right of the legislature to require certain standards for the community to aid in its development as a pleasant place to live. However, to the individual property owner, condemnation of his property for aesthetic reasons represents a serious deprivation of his right to own property.

State highway authorities and state legislative bodies are presented with the problem as to whether they can and should regulate outdoor advertising through the exercise of the power of eminent domain or whether this regulation must be accomplished through the exercise of the state's police power. Illustrative of this dilemma are two cases decided by the New York Court of Appeals. Both cases involved the regulation of billboards. In the first case the New York Superintendent of Public Works asserted authority to condemn negative easements to forbid the erection of signs visible from state highways. His regulations were based on a state law which gave him a general power of eminent domain. In this instance the court ruled that the eminent domain statute did not extend to the prohibition of billboards because it did not specifically or by complication prohibit them. The court also noted the restricted scope of most existing statutes regulating billboards.[1] In the second case the defendant

[1] *Schulman* v. *People*, 203 N.Y.S. 2d 708 (1960).

violated a state statute by placing a billboard within 500 feet of the New York Thruway. The court ruled that this was a proper exercise of the police power as a regulation affecting highway safety.[2]

These two concepts, eminent domain and police power, should not be confused. Eminent domain takes private property for a public use. Compensation is paid for property taken and in many states for property damaged (without regard to whether any is taken), when the taking or damaging is for a public use. Police power is the power inherent in a government to enact laws, within constitutional limits, to promote the order, safety, health, morals and general welfare of the society.

EMINENT DOMAIN

All states have enacted eminent domain statutes designed to facilitate the construction and maintenance of highways. These laws have been drafted in very general terms and usually fail to provide for the regulation of outdoor advertising or the improvement of the scenic view. Existing legislation, therefore, presents a number of problems for state authorities to regulate outdoor advertising. Many of these statutes describe only in general terms the uses where the eminent domain power may be employed. Where statutes contain specific criteria, they usually relate to engineering requirements, such as removal of obstructions, straightening curves and the like.

If states desire to regulate by eminent domain they are confronted with the prevailing notion that the sovereign in the taking of private property for public purposes can take only so much property and only such an interest therein as is necessary for the public purpose to be accomplished. Another objection raised to excess land takings is the power of the sovereign to sell such land to private individuals with restrictions as to future development.

[2] *New York State Thruway Authority* v. *Ashley Motor Court, Inc.*, 218 N.Y.S. 2d 640 (1960).

Ellis v. *Ohio Turnpike Commission*[3] illustrates another attempt to regulate billboards under a broad grant of eminent domain power. As in the New York case the court considered this an attempt to regulate without a specific grant of power and overruled the Commission. The court, however, went on to say that the majority of courts do not answer the question of whether or not condemnation for safety includes billboard regulation. For example, eminent domain may be employed to condemn a safety hazard. However, would it be permissible under the same statute to condemn a sign whose purpose is to distract the driver's attention. State courts consider this a legislative problem that can be answered by specific legislation providing standards that would satisfy the court that administrative power is restrained.

The use of eminent domain as a regulatory device is thus restricted in method by limiting its use to acquire lands, property rights, easements or similar types of interest. Its practical effect seems inadequate because it would be impracticable either to measure the damages for the taking or regulation of property or to provide adequate funds for compensation. However, eminent domain may provide the answer because some courts hold that any time a restriction is placed on private property for a particular public improvement—as distinguished from a regulation based upon public health, safety or morals—the restriction amounts to the taking of an easement and necessitates the payment of compensation.

POLICE POWER

In 1880 the United States Supreme Court stated: "Many attempts have been made in this court to define the police power but never with entire success. It is always easier to determine whether a particular case comes

[3] 120 N.E. 2d 719 (1954).

within the general scope of the power, than to give an abstract definition of the power itself which will be in all respects accurate."[4]

The exercise of police power is limited by the requirements that it be reasonable and not arbitrary and that it be for a legitimate purpose within its scope, and by constitutional prohibitions against the invasion of personal or property rights. These limitations include the requirements that an exercise of the police power serve a public, not a private interest; that it be rationally formulated and administered, and that the means chosen be reasonably related to the desired public purposes. However, a proper police power regulation does not violate constitutional prohibitions even though it may restrain liberty or the use of property. Such an exercise does not constitute a taking or a damaging of property requiring the payment of compensation, even though the value of the property may be greatly reduced as a result of the regulation, as long as the regulation bears a reasonable relationship to the protection and preservation of the public health, safety, morals and general welfare.

THE COURT'S VIEW

The future of any legislation involving the regulation of outdoor advertising depends to a large extent upon the court's view of aesthetics. Most of the health, safety and morals objections to billboards can be overcome in their manner of construction. They can be elevated so as not to collect rubbish or to provide a lurking place for people with evil intent, fireproof structures can be provided, and traffic distractions can be minimized.

The earliest decisions rejected aesthetic considerations as a basis for regulation because of the traditional notion that an individual property owner should be free to use his property in any manner short of being a nuisance. Consequently, the inherent uncertainty of aesthetic prefer-

[4] *Stone* v. *Mississippi,* 101 U.S. 804.

ences made aesthetic standards so uncertain that they were deemed to be outside legitimate police power objectives and as such were considered arbitrary and did not warrant an invasion of property rights under the guise of police power. A state court reasoned: "Aesthetic considerations are a matter of luxury and indulgence rather than of necessity, and it is necessity alone which justifies the exercise of police power to take private property."[5]

A Neat Elevated, Fireproof Structure

Picture Credit:
*Signs of
Our Time*

[5] *City of Passaic v. Paterson Bill Posting Co.*, 72 N.J.L. 285 (1905).

Other courts overturned regulatory legislation because they reasoned that aesthetics were outside the traditional idea of health, safety, morals and welfare. They raised such objections as the difficulty of drafting precise legislation and the possibility of discriminatory enforcements of these statutes.

Later, courts began to acknowledge aesthetic considerations when related to the health, safety or public welfare of the community. "We have reached a point in the development of the police power where an aesthetic purpose needs but little assistance from a practical one in order to withstand an attack on constitutional grounds."[6]

The more recent cases indicate that aesthetic considerations as to purpose and enforcement of regulatory legislation are becoming primary factors which may be considered by the courts. There is no longer a presumption of invalidity of these statutes. Consider the following opinion: "The time has come to make a candid avowal of the right of the legislature to adopt appropriate legislation based upon so called aesthetic but really very practical grounds."[7]

Perhaps the most important single case in this acceptance of aesthetic considerations is *Berman* v. *Parker*,[8] "The concept of the public welfare is broad and inclusive. . . . The values it represents are spiritual as well as physical, aesthetic as well as monetary. It is within the power of the legislature to determine that the community should be beautiful as well as healthy, spacious as well as clean . . ."

Similar pronouncements have been made in state courts concerning aesthetic considerations. A Kentucky court stated: "The obvious purpose of this Act is to enhance the scenic beauty of our roadways. . . . While there may be a public safety interest promoted, the principal objective

[6] *People* v. *Sterling,* 220 N.Y.S. 318.
[7] *Hav-A-Tampa Cigar Co.* v. *Johnson,* 149 Fla. 148.
[8] 348 U.S. 26.

is based upon aesthetic considerations. Though it has been held that such considerations are not sufficient to warrant the invocation of the police power, in our opinion the public welfare is not so limited. . . . The police power is as broad and comprehensive as the demands of society make necessary."[9] An Oregon court reasoned: "We hold that it is within the police power of the city wholly to exclude a particular use if there is a rational basis for its exclusion. . . . The prevention of unsightliness by wholly precluding a particular use within the city may inhibit the growth of the city or frustrate the desires of someone who wishes to make the proscribed use, but the inhabitants of the city have the right to forego the economic gain and the person whose business plans are frustrated is not entitled to have his interest weighed more heavily than the predominant interest of the community."[10]

THE FUTURE

There is no doubt that the law on the extent to which private property may be regulated solely for aesthetic considerations is undergoing development and cannot be said to be conclusively settled.

Since 1937 the United States Supreme Court has not declared a statute regulating economic affairs to be unconstitutional. A majority will uphold state enactments if the facts of the case reveal a basis for the legislation which will commend itself to any reasonable man and aesthetic consideratons represent a reasonable basis for legislation. Therefore, substantive due process is largely a dead issue as far as the regulation of outdoor advertising is concerned.

With the decline of a reliance upon substantive due process courts have had less difficulty relating billboard legislation to the police power, and this trend seems to extend to eminent domain as well. Most states,

[9] *Jasper* v. *Commonwealth*, 375 S.W. 2d 709, 711 (1964).
[10] *Oregon City* v. *Hartke*, 400 P. 2d 255, 261, 262, 263 (1965).

therefore, have enacted legislation regulating billboards in specific areas, with a few prohibiting all signs within prescribed distances from highways. As yet, there appears to be no inclination to regulate all signs visible from highways. It is necessary to examine some of the changes that have occurred with regard to our traditional concepts of property and regulation.

It has been argued that regulations affecting outdoor advertising cannot be sustained because it is not possible to formulate any uniformly applicable standard of scenic beauty which has a rational basis or a relationship to health, morals, safety or welfare. "The exclusion of them [billboards] from regions of natural scenic beauty and historic interest does not exceed the reasonable bounds of the police power. . . . Unusual scenic beauty of the territory as a basis for refusing a permit is sufficiently definite in description to fix a standard in advance for exacting obedience from an applicant. . . . Considerations of taste and fitness may be a proper basis for action in granting and in denying permits for locations for advertising devices."[11]

The billboard is obviously a distracting device. Its purpose and design is intended to divert the attention of the motorist from the highway. This raises the question, does the motorist have the right to be free from distracting sights? If so, does this right interfere with the right of the property owner to advertise? Consider the following opinion of an Ohio court:

> In the instant case, the statutes only deprive the owner of a claimed right to use his land to communicate with those using the highway. . . . any such right can be taken from the landowner without compensation by the state for the purpose of improving the highway as a means of passage for the public. . . . The right asserted is

[11] *General Outdoor Advertising* v. *Department of Public Works,* 193 N.E. 799.

not to own and use land or property to live, to work or to trade. . . . The real and sole value of the billboard is its proximity to the public thoroughfare. Hence, we conceive that the regulation of billboards is not so much a regulation of private property as it is the regulation of the use of streets and other public thoroughfares. . . . In considering the statute weight may be given not only to safety, but also to its effect in promoting comfort, convenience and peace of mind of those using the highway, by removing intrusions on their use.[12]

People v. *Stover*[13] suggests an administrable standard for testing the legitimacy of aesthetic regulations in term of the prohibited activity's effect upon property values. Accurate knowledge of the correlation of aesthetics with property values would enable the courts to determine which aesthetically motivated regulation actually furthers the general welfare.

CONCLUSION

A survey of the decisions involving the regulation of outdoor advertising leads to the conclusion that there is no longer any question about the right to regulate and perhaps even prohibit billboards. It seems certain that the validity of these regulations will depend upon the court's view of aesthetics. In the *Stover* case the court reasoned: "It is settled that conduct which is similarly offensive to the senses of hearing and smell may be a valid subject of regulation under the police power, and we perceived no basis for a different result merely because the sense of sight is involved."[14]

[12] *Ghaster Properties, Inc.* v. *Preston,* 200 N.E. 2d 328 (1964).
[13] 12 N.Y. 2d 462 (1963).
[14] Ibid.

Regulation under the police power would be less expensive and more efficient than eminent domain. However, condemnation may be the only means available in states in which the courts place constitutional limitations on the use of police power for aesthetic purposes.

The amount of compensation to be paid to individual owners would be dependent upon the owner's compensible interest in the land. There is some authority to the extent that this compensible interest may extend only to the right to advertise business conducted on the premises.

From this survey it would seem that the logical basis for any form of regulation of outdoor advertising would be the police power. Some form of permit system would be devised for a reasonable regulation rather than an outright prohibition. Each advertiser would be licensed on a renewable basis and it would be necessary to apply for a permit to construct an advertising device. Although there are many different areas in each state and conditions and circumstances vary, the regulations could consider such items as density of the population, nature of the area to be regulated, proximity of proposed structure to areas of scenic beauty, parks, reservations and the like, proximity of proposed structure to curves, intersections, underpasses, overpasses and other safe areas, and consideration may be given to taste, and fitness as a basis in granting and in denying permits for locations for advertising devices.

"Beauty may not be queen, but she is not an outcast beyond the pale of protection or respect. She may at least shelter herself under the wind of safety, morality, or decency." And with that, the courts leave the aesthetic problem with the legislature.

V. REGULATION OF SIGNS IN THE POST-McLUHAN AGE

Fred P. Bosselman

Zoning originated about 1910 as a result of what might be called a historical accident. There was pressure from a number of sources to keep the living and shopping areas of the upper classes uncontaminated by uses of land that would attract the lower classes. Attempts to use the power of local government to do this were hampered by a rule which the courts had created, the rule of anti-discrimination. This ruling maintained that all regulatory measures must apply uniformly throughout the jurisdiction rather than discriminating in favor of some parts of town or against others. This rule of anti-discrimination meant that if the city fathers wanted to keep tenements and secondhand stores out of the "nice" parts of town they had to keep them out of the rest of town too. This was a very unsatisfactory situation, particularly since many of the city fathers made their living operating tenements and secondhand stores on the other side of the tracks.

Then some lawyers came forth with the idea of dividing the town into districts and creating regulations that applied uniformly within each district. Eventually, after a long battle, the courts agreed and the old anti-discrimination rule was forgotten by most people, and zoning became the way of life.

Perhaps it was all a mistake. Perhaps on that historic day in 1926 when five of the nine Supreme Court judges voted in favor of the City of Euclid, Ohio, it may have been a case of the Court leading us down the wrong path. Perhaps if it had gone the other way we would have been forced into devising more subtle and less discriminatory ways of regulating the use of land—perhaps we would have invented performance standards twenty-five years earlier. But in any event, Euclid won and virtually every city quickly divided itself up into two kinds of districts: the better parts of town and the remainder. In the better parts of town strict regulations were employed to keep out anything that would attract, or even be reminiscent of, those people from the other parts of town. The other parts of town, however, were placed in what I would call "garbage-can districts," in which anything and everything was permitted, except for a few industries that were thought to be so offensive that their odor might even permeate the nice neighborhoods. You know the list: abattoirs, bag-cleaning, ink manufacture, etc.

The courts quickly agreed that signs could be excluded from the nice parts of town, although they had to invent a number of varieties of legal mumbo-jumbo to accomplish it. But the courts could see no justification for regulation of signs in the garbage-can districts because, after all, who cared what happened there? So, if I may overgeneralize a bit but not much, an accommodation was gradually reached between the sign industry and local governments across the country. The signs were kept out of the nice districts and were left to flourish elsewhere. In that way billboards were, like the slums, never seen by the nice people unless they happened to ride a railroad train—and then they pulled down the shades.

The fact that zoning turned out the way it did is primarily due to the fact that zoning was really a creation of the real estate speculators. Its goal was to maximize the value of land for immediate sale. It accomplished that purpose by restricting only those areas where the restrictions would increase the value of land for high-class uses, while opening up property in the rest of the city for virtually any use, thereby increasing its immediate speculative value.

Some of you may think this is a pretty cynical thumbnail sketch of the history of zoning. But while I may be cynical about the past I am optimistic about the future. I am optimistic because I think I see a number of trends running through our society that are changing our entire attitude toward the use of land and changing it for the better.

I would like now to outline briefly a few of these trends as I see them and then show how I think they will cause a dramatic revision in our current attitude toward the regulation of signs.

The first and most important trend that I see is an increased consciousness and sophistication about the need for taking a long-range view of the whole environment rather than merely maximizing the speculative value of property for immediate sale.

While zoning was primarily motivated by the real estate speculator, it has not been immune from other influences over the course of fifty years. Planners, architects, industrial developers and retailers, among others, have witnessed the decline of the city and the threat to urban property values and have come to the realization that the rules that increased the value of property for the real estate speculator often decreased the value of the property for someone who was holding it for long-term investment.

For example, the downtown merchant saw shoppers being attracted to suburban shopping centers by the ability to find parking easily and by the aesthetically pleasant atmosphere of the shopping center. But the typical garbage-can zoning applied to central city business districts was not conducive to encouraging either parking or beauty.

Industrial developers were among the first to see the need for change in the basic philosophy of zoning. Factories located in the old garbage-can districts quickly became obsolete. New land for industry needed tighter restrictions than land for residential use.

A New Technology in
Sign Erection

Picture Credit: *Signs of Our Time*

FRED P. BOSSELMAN

More and more people have begun to see that the long-run value of property depends on the entire city being well-planned and well-run. With this realization of the need for long-range consideration of the whole environment there have come into being a number of new zoning techniques. No longer do you see the so-called "cumulative" zoning ordinance with its garbage-can districts which permitted anything that was permitted in any other district. They have given way to "exclusive zoning" in which districts were zoned for very limited groups of uses. (I think the most amusing example is Los Angeles County's "Arts & Crafts District.") "Performance standards" have come into existence as a way of making equitable distinctions between different types of industry depending on their impact on the total environment. A whole host of so-called "flexible" permit techniques have been created to allow for a much more subtle control over the way in which new uses of land affect their neighbors.

I do not pretend that the new techniques which have resulted from this concern with the total environment have not brought their own problems. But on the whole I think the trend toward what I will call "full environment zoning" is encouraging, and I think it will have a substantial impact on the regulation of signs, as I shall explain in a minute. First, however, I'd like to discuss some other trends that I think I see and then tie them all together.

A corollary of the new concern for a larger environment is a vast increase in our awareness of our environment and a consequent decrease in the attitude of "out of sight, out of mind." With television and high-speed travel nothing is out of sight anymore. We see the slums, not just on an occasional train ride but in the pictures of riots on the nightly TV news. An airplane ride shows us the blankets of smog that covers our cities. Beautifully colored photographs in slick magazines document the slime that flows into our lakes and rivers. New expressways cut through formerly unseen industrial areas and expose to astonished eyes the smoke belching from power plants. (In Chicago there was a direct relationship between the opening of the Stevenson Expressway through the South-west-side industrial area and the sudden concern with air pollution by Commonwealth Edison and the Metropolitan Sanitary District, both of whom have offensive plants adjoining the expressway.) The speed of modern travel exposes our eyes to two, three or ten times the sights our grandfathers saw, and television multiplies this by a factor of hundreds, increasing our awareness of the problems of the world.

As we are more and more made aware of these problems, we have also come to feel that they must be solved, not just ignored. We can ignore them only by turning off our radio and television, staying off the airlines and the expressways, cutting off our magazines and returning to a pastoral way of life—a price that most of us are not willing to pay.

This increased awareness of problems and the increased feeling that problems must be solved also affects the regulation of signs, as I will point out. But television and transportation have had another impact—this one on aesthetics, and this is a third trend I want to discuss.

Recent years have seen great changes in what is accepted as art. The "happening" is the new style in drama. Movies flash from scene to scene with a quickness that requires an exceptional degree of alertness to follow. Expo 67 exposed people to radical new combinations of sight, sound and tactile sensation.

The new technology of the electronic age has created a totally new environment, says Marshall McLuhan. "Each new technology creates an environment that is itself regarded as corrupt and degrading. Yet the new one turns its predecessor into an art form."

The End of a Spectacular Seen from the Highway

Picture Credit: *Signs of Our Time*

Whether you agree with the universality of McLuhan's proposition or not, you cannot deny that commonplace products of the preelectronic age have become popular media of aesthetic expression today. "Superman" has become pop art. Graffiti has become poetry. Auto bodies have become sculpture. Vacuum cleaners have become orchestrated for symphonic music.

Some branches of the advertising industry are rapidly mastering the new aesthetics. The TV commercial has become a highly developed art form. My four-year-old son has developed a delightful capacity for remaining quite oblivious to a blasting TV set until he senses that a commercial has begun—then he switches on his receptors. To his yet uninhibited mind the advertising industry has more clearly grasped the technique of the new media than have the producers of entertainment. Some may scoff and say that this only shows that commercials are composed at the four-year-old's intellectual level. But this would be a misunderstanding of the new aesthetics. The whole direction of the new aesthetics is an attempt to recapture this innocence of youth, this unrestrained wonder at sights and sounds of the child who has not yet been taught that everything from ancient Greece is beautiful while everything "commercial" is ugly.

Having rambled far from my topic, let me now try to come down to earth and tie my subject together by making a few speculations as to how I think the regulation of signs will be affected by the new aesthetics, by the growing awareness of a larger world and by "full environment zoning." While I will gladly concede that these are purely guesses, I will phrase them in the form of predictions in order to give you something definite to shoot at.

1. The existing compromise between the sign industry and government by which signs are permitted in all commercial and industrial areas will

dissolve. Rather, it will gradually fade away as full environment zoning makes it harder and harder to figure out what is or is not a commercial or industrial area. Planned developments increasingly will combine new commercial and residential use without sharp boundaries between them. Industrial parks and office and research zones will be increasingly concerned about maintaining their appearance. If signs are restricted to the old garbage-can zones, they will gradually disappear because the garbage-can zones will gradually disappear. With the new techniques of planning for the full environment it will no longer be possible for signs to slip in unnoticed in the zones with which no one is concerned, because there won't be any such zones left.

The result is that the sign industry is going to have to take a much more positive approach. Instead of "You can let signs in here, it won't hurt much," it will have to be "You should allow signs here; they are desirable because of the following reasons . . ." And the public will need to be given convincing reasons why signs are good.

2. In preparing such reasons the question of "need" will become an increasingly crucial issue. The on-premise/off-premise distinction, which permits signs only if they advertise a product sold on the premises, won't last much longer. This test was devised as a crude way of distinguishing those who "need" to advertise on signs from those who don't. With more and more people traveling the expressways and aware of what's going on, people realize that letting one brand of beer erect a 100-foot illuminated sign because it has a wholesale warehouse underneath it, while prohibiting a competitor from erecting a sign without the warehouse, is an irrational and ineffective method of regulation.

I would venture to predict that the on-premise/off-premise test will be replaced by much more subtle techniques of determining the need which a particular business has to advertise by the use of signs. This question of need is an intricate one, and I don't claim that I would devise a uniformly acceptable definition. Does a motel need to advertise by signs? The motel owner thinks so, but if all motel signs were removed wouldn't the total number of people stopping at motels still remain the same? The distillers say they need to advertise on billboards because they can't get on TV. But is that the type of need to be considered? About the only type of business that I am sure needs to put up signs is an alligator farm —or other such businesses that depend on the impulse shopping of tourists. But some people might say that the tourist should be encouraged to save his dollar. While the definition of need is difficult and may be oppressive, I am afraid that the sign industry's abuse of the on-premise/ off-premise rules will inevitably lead us to stricter and more subtle tests. People's increased awareness of the world around them means they can't be fooled as easily anymore.

Ingenious Use of On-Premise Advertising

Picture Credit: *Signs of Our Time*

3. My first two predictions or hypotheses have sounded ominous for the sign industry. But the third is more hopeful, and it is a simple one: Signs will be "in." The slogan will be "Billboards can be beautiful," by the creator of "Movies are better than ever." If the electric sculpture can be an art form why not the electric sign? Is Charlie Brown advertising a bank on a billboard less artistic than Steve Canyon on canvas in an art museum?

The sign industry is just starting to catch up with the new aesthetics but it is still way behind. The *New Yorker* ran a cartoon a few years ago showing an Andy Warhol-type of artist admiring a new watertower designed to look like a giant Campbell's Soup can. Recently in Minneapolis I saw that a paint company had purchased some obsolete grain elevators and painted them to resemble stacks of cans of its paint. Great advertising, and also a nice twist on McLuhan's famous dictum "the medium is the message."

I would venture a guess—and a hope—that the sign industry will grow increasingly attentive to the aesthetics of their product. Perhaps we will see contests for the funniest sign or the wildest sign. I think the public, too, will become increasingly willing to admit that billboards can be, if not beautiful, at least fun. In one city in which we are working we are trying to draft some regulations which would give the owners of property in an entertainment district a bonus for erecting bigger and better signs. And I can assure you that such regulations are not easy to write. Just picture the city inspector coming out to look at the sign and rejecting it: "Not funny enough."

In summary, I believe that over the next twenty years we will stop thinking of signs as undesirable things that get dumped in with all the other unwanted and ignored uses of land or that get permitted only because we can't figure out a way to prove they aren't needed, and we

A Striking Company Logotype

Picture Credit: *Signs of Our Time*

will start thinking of signs as aesthetic assets which, if well done and in the right place, can amuse us, keep drivers awake and add interest to the environment.

I don't believe the sign industry will succeed in achieving these goals, however, unless it is willing to accept the fact that the public wants a large share of the country free from any signs at all. I think much of the industry is willing to accept this, just as TV advertisers accept limitations on the number of commercials per hour. Our new highways are public assets as much as our radio frequencies or TV channels and equally subject to public regulation. And in both cases it is in the advertiser's interest not to have his message diluted by indiscriminate oversaturation of the viewer's tolerance.

With these future trends in mind I would like to propose to you today a method of regulating highway billboards that, if nothing else, might stimulate you to some thought about a method of billboard regulation that is keyed to the conditions of the 1970's and 1980's.

Suppose that in connection with the construction of a new highway the state were to promulgate regulations prohibiting the construction of billboards on private land at any point within view of the highway. At regular intervals, however, the state would acquire an "island" of land on the fringes of the highway to be devoted to advertising use.

The state would enact regulations regarding the type and size of advertising that could be erected on the island. These regulations might vary considerably from island to island. For example:

1. At some points along the highway "impulse islands" could be created in which the land alongside the highway (and perhaps even over the highway and in the median strip) would be devoted to billboard space for the providers of impulse merchandise, i.e., goods or services that the motorist would not think to ask for but might purchase if the information were made available to him. (Impulse islands, if located at straight stretches where drivers could safely look at the signs, might reduce the danger of driver fatigue by providing a change of pace.) Here the advertiser would be compelled to try to be better or funnier than his neighbor.

2. In some other locations space could be devoted to an information center with "yellow pages" type of advertising. The motorist would be able to turn off the main highway into a special area where, by using a selection of electronic push buttons, he would be able to receive advertising information from all of the providers of a particular category of goods and services, e.g., motels, restaurants, auto repair, etc. Here the advertisers would not be restricted to simple signs but could use movies, sound or perhaps "smellovision" (e.g., "Stop at Joe's for delicious

coffee"). Direct telephone lines could be made available for motel reservations, just as are now provided in many airports.

Title to these "islands" would be conveyed to a quasi-private corporation, the ownership of which would be divided among the owners of the property adjoining the highway as compensation for the loss of their rights to erect signs. The income from sales of advertising rights would be distributed to the shareholders of the corporation, after deducting any cost of administration. In this way the landowners would be compensated for the taking of what would, in effect, be a scenic easement over their lands.

I think it is inevitable that the state governments, and not local governments, will eventually take over sign regulation along expressways. After all, what is more absurd than giving a country town the power to regulate signs directed toward travelers on a highway to which the town may not even have access. I think it is quite feasible politically for the state highway departments to obtain this power because only the state, not the local governments, is in a position to compensate the adjoining landowner for his right to advertise.

In conclusion, I hope that I have made clear my conviction that existing methods of regulating signs are going to change dramatically in the future. Whether you agree with my ideas for change or not, I hope you will agree that the sign industry and government should work together so that signs may become an asset of the community and not a liability.

VI. FEDERAL HIGHWAY BEAUTIFICATION GOALS

Ruth R. Johnson

I believe we all agree on the need for the preservation, restoration, and enhancement of our nation's natural beauty resources, but the question may be "Why do we have a *highway* beautification act?"

President Johnson in his message on natural beauty sent to Congress on February 8, 1965, stated:

> More than any country ours is an automobile society. For most Americans the automobile is a principal instrument of transportation, work, daily activity, recreation and pleasure. By making our roads highways to the enjoyment of nature and beauty we can greatly enrich the life of nearly all of our people in city and countryside alike.
>
> The roads themselves must reflect, in location and design, increased respect for the natural and social integrity and unity of the landscape and the communities through which they pass. (See page 114.)

We have come a long way since the 1930's when our highways were primarily designed to get the country out of the mud (see page 115). Today our superhighways are sophisticated in design and have a far-reaching effect on the type of society in which we live. Unfortunately, the rapid growth of our highway system has brought with it many undesirable side effects. We have all seen the honky-tonk and commercial clutter, commonly called strip development, spread along our major routes. At the other extreme we have seen sterile monotonous superhighways running right through the middle of communities as if they were not there. Thus, the highway beautification program rep-

A Road Which Reflects Unity of Landscape and Design
Picture Credit: *U. S. Bureau of Public Roads*

A Common Hazard of Country Automobile Travel
Picture Credit: *U. S. Bureau of Public Roads*

resents an awakening to the tremendous influence of the highway on its surroundings. As summed up in a publication of the Highway Research Board:[1]

> From the effort to preserve the natural and man-made beauty which is to be seen by the highway traveler, two main lines of benefit result. One group of benefits accrues to the highway itself through more complete achievement of the efficiency, safety, comfort and convenience which planners and designers originally visualized when the highway was laid out. The second group of benefits accrues to the community as a whole by assuring that the highway's influence on its surroundings is not a blighting or divisive one, but rather has an effect of harmonizing the highway with its surroundings and thus stabilizing or enhancing the aesthetic values of the community.

This is why we have the highway beautification program.

HIGHWAY BEAUTIFICATION ACT OF 1965

The Highway Beautification Act of 1965 is the broadest legislation in scope dealing with protection of the highway corridor. This act calls upon the states to control outdoor advertising and junkyards adjacent to Interstate and primary highways and authorizes landscaping and scenic enhancement within the highway corridor.

The outdoor advertising control aspect of the program is not new. In 1958 Congress enacted a voluntary program whereby states which agreed to control outdoor advertising along the Interstate System would be entitled to a bonus payment in the amount of one-half of 1 percent of the cost of the highway project. Originally enacted for three years, it was extended for two-year periods until the second extension ran out

[1] *Roadside Development and Beautification, Legal Authority and Methods,* Part I, National Academy of Sciences, Natural Research Council (1965).

June 30, 1965. At that time only twenty[2] states had agreed to control outdoor advertising along the Interstate System, and because of the upcoming expiration of the bonus program the whole subject of outdoor advertising controls was carefully reconsidered. In May, 1965, the President transmitted to Congress his recommendations to strengthen the control of outdoor advertising, and the Highway Beautification Act of 1965 was signed into law by President Johnson on October 22, 1965.

The 1965 act is, of course, considerably broader and stronger than the 1958 bonus act. Instead of just Interstate highways, the federal-aid primary system is covered as well, adding up to a total of 268,000 miles of highways. As in the 1958 act, actual control of outdoor advertising remains in the hands of the states, and the states may enact and enforce more stringent controls than required under the federal provisions.

Title I of the act stipulates that states must make provision for the control of outdoor advertising within 660 feet of the edge of the right-of-way along all Interstate and primary system highways or lose 10 percent of their federal-aid highway funds (see pages 118–119). Control, however, does not mean elimination of all signs. Advertising signs may be permitted within zoned and unzoned commercial and industrial areas, subject to size, lighting and spacing requirements. In addition, directional and other official signs, including those pertaining to natural wonders and scenic or historic attractions, are permitted outside of commercial and industrial areas. These signs will also be subject to size, lighting and spacing requirements.

The only signs which are not subject to control under the act are "on-premise" signs which are erected on property for the purpose of

[2] Five additional states entered into agreement before the program expired bringing the total to twenty-five states; they are: California, Colorado, Connecticut, Delaware, Georgia, Hawaii, Illinois, Iowa, Kentucky, Maine, Maryland, Nebraska, New Hampshire, New Jersey, New York, North Dakota, Ohio, Oregon, Pennsylvania, Rhode Island, Vermont, Virginia, Washington, West Virginia and Wisconsin.

Illustrations of Typical Highway Blight

advertising its sale or lease or for advertising an activity conducted on the property (see pages 120–121). Along the Interstate System, and within the right-of-way, the act permits states to provide signs to inform travelers of specific services available at approaching interchanges. These signs will replace the gas, food, lodging signs and will mention brand names of gasoline, restaurants and motels. The states may also provide maps, informational directories, advertising pamphlets and information centers at safety rest areas (see page 122).

A Variety of Services Are Advertised

Picture Credit: *U. S. Bureau of Public Roads*

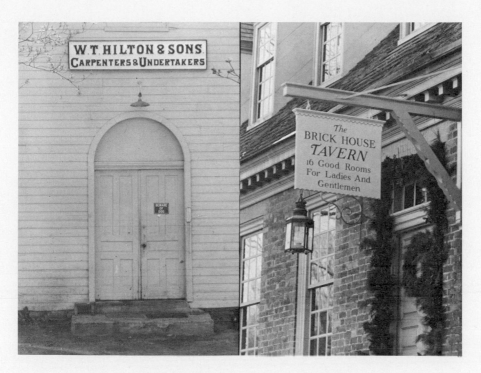

Specific Services Are Advertised Here

Picture Credit: *U. S. Bureau of Public Roads*

Outdoor advertising signs which were legally in existence on September 1, 1965, but which are not in conformity with the requirements may be allowed to remain until July 1, 1970. Other signs lawfully erected which do not conform to the requirements may be allowed to remain for as long as five years from the date they become nonconforming before they are required to be removed.

The State of Texas Informs Travellers

Picture Credit: *U. S. Bureau of Public Roads*

Finally, the act provides that under certain conditions owners of signs and property owners shall receive compensation from the state if they are required to remove signs from controlled areas. The federal government will reimburse the states for 75 percent of the compensation costs they incur. The compensation features of the act are mandatory upon every state as a condition to receiving the full amount of federal-aid highway funds.

While junkyard control under the Highway Beautification Act of 1965 established a precedent of federal interest in this area, it by no means introduced such control in the states. Shortly after the act was passed a questionnaire was sent to the states to determine the extent of their existing authority for controlling junkyards. It was learned that twenty-three states at that time had statutes controlling the location or requiring the screening of junkyards on a statewide basis. The response also indicated forty-six states could control junkyards in municipalities or other political subdivisions by zoning, licensing or other legal methods, and twenty-eight states had some legal method of controlling junkyards outside of municipalities.

The junkyard control features under Title II of the federal act require the states to make provision for the effective control of the establishment and maintenance of junkyards within 1,000 feet of the edge of the right-of-way along all Interstate and primary system highways or

An Ironical Welcome to a Big City

Picture Credit: *U. S. Bureau of Public Roads*

The Sad Debris Point to the Necessity of Junkyard Control

Picture Credit: *U. S. Bureau of Public Roads*

lose 10 percent of their federal-aid highway funds (see pages 123–124). We should note here that there is a difference between the control areas of the outdoor advertising and junkyard laws. The control area for junkyards is 1,000 feet from the edge of the right-of-way, while the outdoor advertising law extends only to 660 feet. However, like the outdoor advertising law, control of junkyards does not mean their elimination. Under the act, junkyards must be screened or otherwise removed from sight unless they are located in zoned or unzoned industrial areas. Junkyards which were lawfully in existence on October 22, 1965, and which the Secretary finds as a practical matter cannot be screened are not required to be removed until July 1, 1970. Under certain conditions, junkyard owners shall receive compensation from the state for the removal, relocation or disposal of their junkyards. Such compensation is also mandatory, and federal funds will reimburse the states for 75 percent of their compensation costs. Additionally, federal funds may be used to pay 75 percent of a state's cost of landscaping and screening junkyards.

A True Scenic Enhancement

Picture Credit: *U. S. Bureau of Public Roads*

Landscaped Highways Preserve Natural Beauty

Picture Credit: *U. S. Bureau of Public Roads*

126 RUTH R. JOHNSON

Magnificent Sight at a Rest Stop

Picture Credit: *U. S. Bureau of Public Roads*

FEDERAL HIGHWAY BEAUTIFICATION GOALS 127

Title III, the scenic enhancement section of the act, is now thirty years old. Originating in the Federal-Aid Highway Act of 1938, it began by authorizing landscaping and roadside development as a part of the normal costs of highway construction (see pages 125–126). In 1940, the act was amended to add the concept of land acquisition for preservation of natural beauty within the highway corridor (see page 127). Importantly, it also introduced the use of 100 percent federal funds for this latter purpose. This section of the 1965 act is subdivided into two parts. The first provides that the Secretary may approve the costs of landscape and roadside development as a part of the construction costs of federal-aid highways. The second section provides for an allocation of funds equivalent to three percent of federal-aid highway funds apportioned to a state for landscape and roadside development within the right-of-way and for the acquisition of interests in and improvement of

A Scenically Beautiful Recreation Area

Picture Credit: *U. S. Bureau of Public Roads*

adjacent strips of land necessary for the restoration, preservation and enhancement of scenic beauty, including the acquisition and development of publicly owned rest and recreation areas and sanitary and other facilities within or adjacent to the highway right-of-way (see pages 128–129). These funds are not required to be matched by the states.

This latter portion of the program is broad and flexible. It may include simple tree-thinning to open a scenic vista, or an easement to preserve a natural setting or to take advantage of unusual man-made beauty, such as a cityscape or an elaborate safety rest area designed with adequate buildings, sanitary facilities, picnic areas, hiking trails and other recreational facilities (see page 130). The goal here is to provide areas within the highway corridor which are not only visually attractive but which consider the human element, so that people can actively use and enjoy some of these surroundings (page 131).

Public Rest Areas Can Be Made Attractive

Picture Credit: *U. S. Bureau of Public Roads.*

Scenic Highways Beautified by Planning and Landscaping

Picture Credit: *U. S. Bureau of Public Roads*

130 RUTH R. JOHNSON

A Quiet Rest Stop under the Tree

Picture Credit: *U. S. Bureau of Public Roads*

STATE IMPLEMENTATION

It must be remembered, however, that unless the states elect to carry out a program in compliance with the federal provisions, the federal act is meaningless and can have only the negative effect of the loss of certain federal-aid funds. Thus, in the last analysis, it is state action which makes the program operational.

First, the states need enabling legislation. Since the passage of the federal act, thirty-two states have enacted some type of legislation relating to outdoor advertising; forty-one states have enacted junkyard control legislation, and forty-three states have enacted laws relating to landscaping and scenic enhancement.

Next, a state will have to provide for the implementation of its own legislation. Here are the "gears" by which the program is enforced and made applicable to the citizens of a state. At this stage, and throughout the program, the operational aspects and the enforcement measures at both the state and federal level should complement each other.

FEDERAL IMPLEMENTATION

At the federal level, the Bureau of Public Roads, acting under the Federal Highway Administration has been charged with the responsibility of administering the act. Prior to the creation of the Department of Transportation on April 1, 1967, it was the responsibility of the Bureau of Public Roads under the Department of Commerce.

Shortly after the passage of the act, the Secretary of Commerce and the Bureau of Public Roads called for a series of meetings with the states and interested groups to explain the Highway Beautification Act and to discuss some of its plans to carry it out. Almost simultaneously, the Bureau was proceeding to arrange for the fifty-two public hearings[3]

[3] One in each state, the District of Columbia and Puerto Rico.

called for under Section 303 of the act for the purpose of gathering all relevant information on which to base the standards, criteria, rules and regulations required.

The standards and criteria pertaining to outdoor advertising covered the definition of an unzoned commercial or industrial area, and the size, lighting and spacing of signs permitted in commercial and industrial zones and areas, all of which must be determined by agreement between the Secretary and the several states. In addition, it covered the national standards which must be promulgated by the Secretary for outdoor advertising controls on public lands and reservations of the United States, for directional and other official signs and notices off the right-of-way, and for official highway signs within Interstate rights-of-way giving specific information to the traveling public.

On January 28, 1966, draft standards and criteria were published in the Federal Register for six categories of standards, criteria, rules and regulations called for under the act. These draft standards and criteria were for the specific purpose of providing a frame of reference for discussion purposes and all parties were advised that they did not represent conclusions or even tentative conclusions on the part of Public Roads or the Secretary.

Most of the information received from the public hearings pertained to the control of outdoor advertising. The hearings were completed in May, 1966, and the testimony amounted to about 20,000 pages. In addition, written statements, often supplemented with exhibits, numbered about 1,500. As each hearing transcript was received it was reproduced together with the exhibits, and copies were sent to the state highway departments and the subcommittees on roads of the Senate and House Public Works Committees. Teams of Bureau personnel evaluated all of the testimony and prepared staff recommendations of standards and criteria for consideration by the Administration and the states.

In early July, 1966, proposed standards and criteria were given wide dissemination, and all interested groups, organizations and individuals were invited to comment and make recommendations. Beginning in mid-July, extensive, detailed and critical comments and recommendations were received by Public Roads concerning the July proposals. Almost without exception, the comments described the proposals as either too lax or too strict, depending on the writer's point of view. Outdoor advertising associations and companies claimed the criteria would idle large segments of each and every company's plant, labor unions predicted widespread unemployment in the industry, and conservation and beautification groups termed the proposals a sellout to the "powerful billboard lobby." During October, the Public Roads staff considered all of the comments which had been received concerning the July proposals, together with other relevant information, whether previously known or newly available. Revised proposed standards and criteria were developed, and all of this material was reported to Congress in January of 1967 as required under the act.

From April to June, 1967, the Subcommittees on Roads of the Senate and House Public Works Committees held hearings to consider H.R. 7797 and S. 1467 which would authorize federal funds to carry out the highway beautification program and at that time reviewed the entire program and the manner in which it was being administered.

During this time there was a lot of talk that the Highway Beautification Act of 1965 would be amended and that no money would be provided to carry it out. Bills were introduced which would eliminate mandatory just compensation for the removal of nonconforming signs and junkyards, and others would have substituted a scenic area approach instead of the present statutory process for the control of outdoor advertising and junkyards. The Secretary of Transportation made the Department's views clear on both points. In his testimony before the Senate Sub-committee on Roads of June 28, 1967, he stated that "Compensation for a loss suffered by an individual in the interest of a broad public benefit is a long-accepted principle which the Administration fully endorses. We feel that the provisions of the act, as written, provide the most equitable approach." Regarding the scenic area bills, he concluded his comments with this premise: "If we can accept the fact that our Interstate and primary system highways, with the exception of zoned and unzoned commercial and industrial areas, are worthy of protection, I think you will agree that the Highway Beautification Act as written is a scenic area law."

It has been said that we cannot afford to meet both our domestic needs and our foreign commitments and still be concerned with the quality of our environment, which includes, among other things, the appearance of the roadside. Since the highway beautification program represents approximately 1 percent of the total monies spent on road-building in the United States, it was the Administration's view that this is but a small price to pay to preserve the American roadsides and landscapes.

Secretary Boyd expressed this thought in these words:

> It has been said by some that we cannot afford beauty for our highways yet, that other demands for the tax dollar are more important. . . . We not only can but we must. Whether in the open spaces of our cities or through our national historical sites, through our rural fields or over the mountains of our wilderness, preservation of beauty along our highways can no longer be classified as a frill, to be added or dropped at leisure. It has become an integral part of the highway planning and improvement process. Just as surely as beauty is a superlative quality which surpasses precise definition, so is it an impossible quality on which to place a price tag. This is not true of ugliness. We know something about

the high price of ugliness. It is an expensive condition, not simply in the terms of blight it casts on the human spirit and climate, but also in the spiraling cost of its elimination. Unlike beauty, ugliness spreads if left unchecked, and its removal costs spread accordingly. Often it secures so strong a foothold that the natural beauty it has destroyed can never be fully restored, at any price. This is the high penalty of neglect—a penalty foreseen when this Act was created, a penalty spared for our children if this Act is carried out. For this Act recognizes that natural beauty is just as basic a national resource as are air, water, forests, and mineral deposits, and must just as surely be safeguarded from depletion and destruction.[4]

I do not wish to imply that the objectives of the Highway Beautification Act erased or minimized the many problems presented in implementing the act because it is a far-reaching and complex law not easily understood in all of its ramifications and certainly not easily administered to the satisfaction of all affected or interested parties. The outdoor advertising aspects of the program obviously stirred up the most problems and raised probably the most widespread misunderstanding of the federal role in this connection. Most people will recall that the guidelines for size, lighting and spacing of signs in commercial and industrial areas and definition of an unzoned commercial and industrial area as reported to Congress were mistaken for national standards. It became very difficult to clarify the fact that the Secretary was not unilaterally promulgating standards in this area, and that the act itself clearly requires these items to be determined by agreement with the several states. Perhaps some of the reason for this misunderstanding resulted from the language of the act itself which does call for the promulgation of national standards in three other subsections concerning outdoor advertising controls. Added to this, Sections 302 and 303 of the act

[4] In testimony before the Subcommittee on Roads of the House Public Works Committee, May 2, 1967, considering H.R. 7797 (p. 932 of the Hearings).

required the Secretary to report to Congress not later than January 10, 1967, the results of a detailed estimate of the cost of carrying out the act, the results of a comprehensive study of the economic impact of the act and the standards, criteria, rules and regulations to be applied in carrying out the outdoor advertising and junkyard control provisions. Each of these was to some extent dependent on one or both of the other two and all were closely interrelated. Without knowing a standard for outdoor advertising control to be applied in a state, it is, of course, impossible to predict the cost of outdoor advertising control or the economic impact of such control. This is why, in our opinion, guidelines for commercial and industrial areas were required to be developed and reported to Congress.

The Administration's position regarding the negotiation of agreements with the states was also clarified in a letter dated May 24, 1967, from Secretary Boyd to Mr. Kluczynski, chairman of the House Subcommittee on Roads. Basically it set forth four points. First, that state zoning determinations with respect to zoned commercial and industrial areas would be accepted. Second, concerning unzoned commercial and industrial areas, the Department shall be happy to request the guidance and suggestions of the several states. The only absolute requirement the Department would insist upon would be the existence of at least one commercial activity in any such area. Third, with regard to the determination of what constitutes customary use in the zoned commercial and industrial areas, the Department shall be glad to look to the states for certification that either the state authority or a bona fide local zoning authority has made such a determination. In unzoned commercial and industrial areas, the Department will recognize local practice on customary use as mutually agreed to by state and federal agencies. It will be the Department's policy to assume the good faith of the several states in this regard. The only exception made to these points by the Secretary

Some Examples of Attractive Information Centers

Picture Credit: *U. S. Bureau of Public Roads*

would be in a situation where a state or local authority might attempt to circumvent the law by zoning an area as commercial for outdoor advertising purposes only. The fourth point states that what is determined in good faith by a bona fide local or state zoning authority as customary use will be an acceptable basis for standards as to size, spacing and lighting in the commercial and industrial areas within the geographical jurisdiction of that state or local authority.

It is believed that the hearings held by the House and Senate Subcommittees on Roads in the spring and early summer of 1967 and the communications of Secretary Boyd did much to clear the air on these areas of misunderstanding, even though no funds were authorized to carry out the program for the fiscal year ending June 30, 1968. S. 1467 was passed by the Senate and recommended for passage by the House Public Works Committee, but the bill never reached the House floor for action. However, after the House hearings eighteen states and the District of Columbia entered into agreements with the Secretary to control outdoor advertising, an accomplishment which prior to that time would have been impossible.

In the spring of 1968, the House and Senate once again considered authorizations for the highway beautification program as part of the Federal-Aid Highway Act of 1968. The Senate bill (S. 3418) made no substantive amendments to the Highway Beautification Act and authorized a total of $255,000,000 program funds. The House amended the bill to take all of the teeth out of the program and provided no funds. The bill then went to conference, and the final bill as passed by the House and Senate made three minor amendments and authorized program funds for fiscal year 1970 in the following amounts: $2,000,000 for outdoor advertising control, $3,000,000 for junkyard control, and $20,000,000 for landscaping and scenic enhancement, or a total of $25,000,000. Additionally, $1,250,000 was provided for administrative expenses for fiscal years 1969 and 1970. The bill was signed into law by President Johnson on August 23, 1968. Significantly, one of the amendments provides that whenever a bona fide state, county or local zoning authority has made a determination of customary use, such determination will be accepted in lieu of control by agreement in the zoned commercial and industrial areas within the geographical jurisdiction of such authority. The conference report states that this provision sets forth by statute the method of administration of the act as outlined in the Secretary's letter of May 24, 1967, a provision which is contained in many of the agreements executed with the states prior to this latest Congressional action. Thus, it appears that a slow evolutionary process has been taking place whereby all affected parties are gaining a better understanding of the program, not only toward its implementation generally, but toward the effect and impact of specific provisions as well.

TECHNICAL ASPECTS OF THE PROGRAM

To provide an idea of some of the technical aspects of the program, perhaps one of its most complex and difficult to understand concepts concerns the legal implications of the act upon existing state control laws. As mentioned earlier, the federal act does not in and of itself directly regulate outdoor advertising or junkyards; this depends upon state or local law. The federal act is meaningless without state legislation to carry it out.

By the same token, all existing state laws remain in full force and effect until a state takes legislative action otherwise. The federal act in no way supersedes state laws, or local laws for that matter.

A recent Supreme Court decision in the State of Washington[5] dealing with a state outdoor advertising control law expressed it this way:

[5] *Markham Advertising Company, Inc.* v. *The State of Washington*, 439 P 2nd 248.

Our examination of §131, (of Title 23 U.S.C.) leads us to conclude that its essential operation is to condition payment of 10 per cent of a state's share of federal-aid highway funds upon the state's exercise of its powers to regulate outdoor advertising in a manner consistent with federal standards. We think that the purpose of the federal statute is obviously to induce the states to act, not to require them to do so. The statute allows the state to choose between foregoing 10 per cent of its allotment of federal-aid highway funds and compliance. . . . We hold that Congress has not invoked the Supremacy Clause by pre-empting the field of regulation covered by the state Act; that 23 U.S.C. §131 (Supp. II, 1967) is directory, and does not interfere with the application of the Act as written.

We see then, that the federal act and the regulations promulgated thereunder represent the guides to be followed by the states as a condition to full participation in federal-aid funds. Thus, even without the express language which Congress incorporated in the act under Subsection 131(k) which provides for stricter controls by the states, the states could not have been precluded from adopting more restrictive controls.

To illustrate this point, we have been asked on several occasions if the July 1, 1970, removal date for signs lawfully in existence on September 1, 1965, would preclude a state from removing such signs at an earlier date. Obviously, the answer is no. The federal act simply contemplates that these signs will not remain after July 1, 1970.

As a corollary, the just compensation features of the act and the federal requirements adopted thereunder are simply a limitation on federal participation, but the states may pay for whatever items they deem necessary under their laws. Based on this principle, it can be readily seen that a state could pay for the removal of the so-called interim signs (i.e., those erected between October 22, 1965, and January 1, 1968) even though the federal act itself does not provide for federal funds to be used in removing such signs.

The next major question concerning existing control laws involves the bonus agreements with the twenty-five states which elected to control outdoor advertising along the Interstate System under the 1958 act. The language of the act as amended, provides basically that:

> Any State highway department which has . . . entered into an agreement with the Secretary to control the erection and maintenance of outdoor advertising signs, displays, and devices in areas adjacent to the Interstate System shall be entitled to receive bonus payments *as set forth in the agreement,* but no such State highway department shall be entitled to such payments *unless* the State *maintains the control required under such agreement.* . . . The provisions of this subsection *shall not be construed to exempt any State from controlling outdoor advertising as otherwise provided in this section.*

This section was amended by the 1968 act to provide bonus payments to those states having 1958 bonus agreements so long as they maintain the control required by the 1958 act, irrespective of what controls are required by the 1965 act. Under the language as originally written, a bonus state was required to maintain the control required under the bonus agreement or the control under the 1965 act, whichever was stricter, to be entitled to bonus payments after January 1, 1968.

ACCOMPLISHMENTS

Many will be interested in learning what has been accomplished to date.

As far as billboard control agreements are concerned, eighteen states[6]

[6] Rhode Island, Vermont, Virginia, Hawaii, Connecticut, New York, Kentucky, Minnesota, Maine, Utah, Puerto Rico, California, Maryland, Alaska, Pennsylvania, Delaware, Iowa, Ohio.

and the District of Columbia had entered into agreements as of September 1, 1968. We are now in active negotiation with most of the other states, several of which have submitted agreements that are being reviewed at this moment. The terms of the executed agreements have been tailored to meet the needs of the individual states and vary so widely from state to state that it would be difficult to explain these in detail. The two most important provisions at the present time are the local control provisions in the zoned commercial or industrial areas and a "grandfather clause" which permits signs lawfully in existence within commercial or industrial areas prior to the time the agreement is executed to remain even though they may not meet the requirements. This means that the size, lighting and spacing requirements apply only to future signs in such areas. Needless to say this provision will minimize the impact on the outdoor advertising industry and will greatly simplify administration at the state level.

The most significant strides have been made in implementing the junkyard control and landscaping and scenic enhancement programs. Many states have done a fine job of gearing up for these important programs. In fact, more than 4,000 projects have been authorized and the states have been able to obligate virtually all of the funds made available to them.

In addition, since March 1965, the states have obligated another $239,000,000 of regular federal-aid funds as a part of normal construction for such things as landscaping, erosion control, development of roadside rest areas and screening of unsightly areas.

We have been particularly pleased with the various efforts made in the states to provide the motorist with information within and without the right-of-way other than through the use of advertising signs.

Many are familiar with the experiment of using motorist information signs within the right-of-way on Interstate 95 in Virginia. This was a cooperative project between the Bureau of Public Roads and the state.

These signs contained the symbol of gasoline companies as well as names of food and lodging establishments.

While not fully accepted by all state highway officials, they proved to be popular with the traveling public and their value is being carefully examined at the present time.

The information or sign plazas located in rest areas off the traveled portion of the highway and not readable from the roadway itself have likewise been popular and afford an opportunity to give more detailed information concerning available roadside services to the traveling public. The value of signing plazas for the motorist is also under study.

The Highway Beautification Act, under Title I states: "A State may also establish information centers at safety rest areas for the purpose of informing the public of places of interest within the State and providing such other information as a state may consider desirable."

The Elegant Information Center of the State of Louisiana

Picture Credit: *U. S. Bureau of Public Roads*

Iowa Provides Interesting Traveller Information

Picture Credit: *U. S. Bureau of Public Roads*

It is our policy to encourage the use of information centers at safety rest areas, as we believe that this can be an effective method of providing the traveling public with the full information which it needs and desires. These information centers are becoming increasingly popular with the traveling public and state highway officials (see page 138). The State of Louisiana, for example, has opened a most impressive tourist information center for the motoring public (see page 144).

The State of Iowa now has two tourist information centers called "Infosites" located in the eastern part of the state and provided through the cooperation of government and private industry (see pages 145–146).

Iowa Was the First State To Open an "Infosite"

Picture Credit: *U. S. Bureau of Public Roads*

The construction of these information centers has been financed by the state highway department on the condition that the cost be reimbursed by "Infosite" over a period of years through an arrangement whereby the center is leased to Infosite. We have recently learned of an imaginative plan in Vermont to provide information centers with central telephone service, plus other sources of tourist information that include an idea for official signs on the right-of-way using symbols for services available in the area.

We are very enthusiastic about information centers for the traveling public, particularly since this concept lends itself to the utilization of so many new and imaginative approaches.

The Highway Stretches Far

Picture Credit: *U. S. Bureau of Public Roads*

We believe that we are making real progress demonstrating that the act is being implemented in the public interest. As in 1965, we still believe that Congress enacted a good, workable program that can and should be carried out in cooperation and partnership with the states in the best tradition of the federal-aid program.

We in the Federal Highway Administration and the Bureau of Public Roads stand ready to assist in every way possible in achieving the goals of highway beautification.

It is indeed a wonderful challenge, and our goal is to move forward on programs that will be meaningful to the American motorist today and to our children tomorrow (see pages 147–148).

Beautification Is Achieved Here

Picture Credit: *U. S. Bureau of Public Roads*

VII. FEDERAL HIGHWAY BEAUTIFICATION: OUTDOOR ADVERTISING CONTROL, LEGISLATION AND REGULATION

Clifton W. Enfield

Over the years, advertising has been both condemned and eulogized. By some, it has been characterized as an insult to the intelligence of thinking men. Others profess that advertising is a necessary and desirable catalyst of our private enterprise system, which has produced the world's highest standard of living and is fundamental to the American way of life.

Thomas Jefferson, either to praise advertising or to criticize news reporting, once said, "Advertising contains the only truths to rely on in a newspaper." Whereas, Stephen Leacock is credited with the quip that "Advertising may be described as the science of arresting human intelligence long enough to get money from it."

Unfortunately, such widely divergent views, which persist today, thrust any consideration of the regulation of advertising into an arena of great controversy, where the participants have deep and sincere feelings, which are often as much the product of emotions as of objective thinking.

Since 1955 there has emerged from this smoldering fire of public opinion a steadily growing demand for the regulation of outdoor advertising adjacent to the nation's highways. More and more people have become convinced that if the safety and enjoyment of highway travel are to be promoted, there must be realistic and effective control of billboards and on-premise advertising.

Practically everyone favors beautifying our highways, including some kind of regulation of outdoor advertising. Generalizations are easily stated, but serious difficulties are encountered when we get down to specifics. The hard core of the problem is twofold: First, what is realistic and effective control of outdoor advertising? And, second, how can it best be accomplished?

For a better understanding of what is involved in these two considerations, as a basis for making suggestions for solutions to the perplexing problem of advertising control, we should be intimately familiar with the legislative and administrative actions taken by the federal government in this field in recent years. Time does not permit a detailed discussion of the subject, including all of the alternatives considered and the reasons for selecting certain ones and rejecting others. But I do wish to trace the history of federal efforts to control outdoor advertising, for the purpose of showing how the federal interest developed and discussing the methods of control adopted.

EARLY CONGRESSIONAL INTEREST IN ADVERTISING CONTROL

In 1955, the Senate Committee on Public Works approved an amendment by Senator Richard L. Neuberger (D-Ore.) to a bill for enactment of the Federal-Aid Highway Act of 1955 (S. 1048, 84th Congress, 1st Session). The amendment would permit the Secretary of Commerce to acquire exclusive advertising rights on lands adjoining certain rights-of-way of the Interstate System for a distance not exceeding 500 feet from the highway right-of-way. This provision applied only to those states which did not have legal authority to acquire rights-of-way with control of access necessary for this system of federal-aid highways. The Secretary would acquire the advertising rights at the same time he acquired the right-of-way and access control, for subsequent conveyance to the states. The provision was deleted from the bill on the floor of the Senate, and no further action was taken on the bill after it passed the Senate.

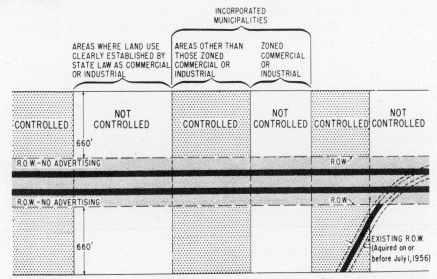

Drawing Illustrates the Application of the Various Provisions of the Highway Act of 1958

Picture Credit: *U. S. Bureau of Public Roads*

Highway legislation was revived the following year, and the Federal-Aid Highway Act of 1956 (P.L. 627, 84th Congress, 2nd Session) was enacted. This act did not contain any provision for the control of advertising. However, enactment of the 1956 act, which provided for completion of the Interstate System, gave impetus and direction to the efforts of those sincerely concerned with the need for roadside advertising control.

In an article appearing in the December, 1956, issue of *Harper's Magazine,* Mr. Robert Moses deplored the lack of provision for advertising control in the Federal-Aid Highway Act of 1956. Public response to this article, and to other magazine and newspaper articles, was enthusiastic in support of the control of advertising and stimulated further consideration of the matter.

When Secretary of Commerce Sinclair Weeks appeared before the Subcommittee on Public Roads of the Senate Committee on Public Works on January 7, 1957, he called attention to the widespread feeling throughout the country that advertising adjacent to the 41,000-mile Interstate System should be restricted in order to preserve the natural beauty and pleasing character of the natural landscape and in the interest of highway safety. He further pointed out that additional legislation would be required if such is to be accomplished and advised that the matter, which presented many complexities, was then under study by the Department of Commerce.

Later in January of 1957, Senator Neuberger introduced a bill (S. 963, 85th Congress, 1st Session) to require the Secretary of Commerce to publish recommended national policy standards for the control of signs in areas within 500 feet of the right-of-way of the Interstate System. The standards would limit signs in such areas to:

1. highway directional signs and official notices;
2. signs for the sale or lease of property on which they are located, and
3. signs in any commercial area adjacent to and accessible from an Interstate highway and advertising a business conducted within such commercial area.

To encourage the states to carry out the national policy, Senator Neuberger's bill provided that federal-aid highway funds could partici-

Class 1 Sign. Directional or Other Official Signs or Notices

Picture Credit: *U. S. Bureau of Public Roads*

pate in the costs of acquiring interests in land to control advertising. Similar bills were introduced in the House of Representatives.

On March 18, 1957, the Senate Subcommittee on Public Roads commenced hearings on Senator Neuberger's bill. Secretary Weeks testified on the need and desirability of such legislation and submitted a draft of a bill proposed by the Department of Commerce for the control of advertising. The Department's draft bill provided that the federal share of the cost of any Interstate highway project in any state which did not agree to carry out the national policy for the control of advertising would be decreased 5 percent, which generally would reduce the federal share from 90 percent to 85 percent of the cost of projects. This proposed legislation prohibited all outdoor advertising within 750 feet of the Interstate System, except:

1. directional and other official signs;
2. signs advertising the sale or lease of property on which they are located;
3. signs advertising activities being conducted upon the property on which such signs are located, and
4. signs on land actually zoned commercial or industrial.

The draft bill did not authorize the Secretary to promulgate standards for regulation of signs permitted under the bill.

At the close of the hearings in April, 1957, Senator Albert Gore (D-Tenn.), chairman of the Subcommittee, indicated that he detected a reluctance on the part of the members of the Subcommittee to penalize states. He suggested using a "carrot" rather than a "stick" by providing an incentive to the states to accomplish the desired goal, rather than assessing a penalty for failure to control advertising.

At the request of the Subcommittee, the Department of Commerce prepared a draft substitute bill which eliminated all penalties and provided for an increase of three-fourths of 1 percent in the federal share of the costs of Interstate highway projects for which agreements were entered into to control advertising within 750 feet of the Interstate System. This bill provided that such agreements would limit signs to:

1. directional or other official signs;
2. signs advertising the sale or lease of property on which they are located;
3. signs advertising activities conducted upon the property on which the signs are located, and

Class 2 Signs, Not Prohibited by State Law, Advertise Activities
Conducted on the Property Where Signs Are Located

Picture Credit: *U. S. Bureau of Public Roads*

FEDERAL HIGHWAY BEAUTIFICATION: OUTDOOR ADVERTISING CONTROL 155

4. signs that are in the public interest and which, by reason of their location, frequency, or character, do not impair the safety of travel or interefere with enjoyment of the natural beauty of the area through which the highway passes, except that the total mileage of the Interstate System in any state from which signs may be viewed shall not exceed 2 percent of the total mileage of the system in such state.

On May 24, 1957, the Senate Subcommittee on Public Roads published a committee print of an amendment to Senator Neuberger's original bill (S. 963), which amendment was generally similar in concept to the draft substitute bill prepared by the Department of Commerce at the request of the Subcommittee. The principal differences were that the committee print required the Secretary to publish recommended standards for the control of advertising, decreased the controlled area from 750 feet to 600 feet (which is ten chains, or one furlong, or forty rods, or one-eighth mile), and increased from 2 percent to 5 percent the total Interstate highway mileage within a state from which off-premise signs could be viewed.

The Senate Committee on Public Works asked the Department of Commerce for its views on the committee print. By letter dated June 28, 1957, Secretary Weeks advised the Committee that the Department was in accord with the objectives of the print relating to advertising control and would interpose no objections to its enactment, but that he was convinced the proposed legislation submitted by the Department in January of 1957 would accomplish the objective most effectively. The Secretary further pointed out that the committee print provided for advertising control on a project-by-project basis rather than on a state-wide basis and that statewide control would be preferable. No further action was taken by the Committee during the remainder of 1957.

FEDERAL-AID HIGHWAY ACT OF 1958

Early in 1958, Senator Prescott Bush (R-Conn.) and Senator Thomas Kuchel (R-Calif.) introduced bills to control advertising adjacent to the Interstate System. Senator Bush's bill (S. 3041, 85th Congress, 2d Session) was similar to the Senate committee print of May 24, 1957, except it provided that federal-aid funds could participate in the costs of interests in land acquired to control advertising in amounts not to exceed 3 percent of the federal share payable on account of any project.

Senator Kuchel's bill (S. 3218, 85th Congress, 2d Session) provided for a 1 percent bonus in the federal share of the cost of Interstate projects to which the national policy for the control of advertising is applied. The national policy would have prohibited all advertising within 660 feet of the main traveled way of the Interstate System located upon any right-of-way acquired after July 1, 1956, except:

1. signs inside of incorporated municipalities;
2. directional and other official signs;
3. signs advertising the sale or lease of the property upon which they are located;
4. signs advertising activities being conducted upon the property on which such signs are located, and
5. signs erected or maintained pursuant to specific authorizing state or local laws or regulations.

In March of 1958, the Senate Subcommittee on Public Roads held a hearing on Senator Bush's bill, Senator Kuchel's bill and Senator Neuberger's bill, as amended by the committee print.

In the meantime, the House Committee on Public Works held hearings in January and February of 1958 on a bill (H.R. 9821, 85th Congress, 2d Session) by Representative George H. Fallon (D-Md.) to authorize the appropriation of funds for highway construction. Advertising control was not considered in those House hearings. On March 6, 1958, the House Committee reported its bill, to enact the Federal-Aid Highway Act of 1958, to the House of Representatives (H.R. 9821, Union Calendar No. 577; House Report No. 1591, 85th Congress, 2d Session). It was passed by the House on March 13, 1958, and sent to the Senate. The measure, as it passed the House, contained no advertising control provisions.

The Senate Committee on Public Works marked up its own bill to enact the Federal-Aid Highway Act of 1958, introduced by Senator Gore, and reported it to the Senate on March 22, 1958 (S. 3414, Calendar No. 1432; Senate Report No. 1407, 85th Congress, 2d Session). Section 12 of the reported Senate bill contained certain provisions for the control of outdoor advertising, including features of each of the bills introduced by Senators Neuberger, Bush, and Kuchel.

This section established a national policy to regulate the erection and maintenance of outdoor advertising within 660 feet of the edge of the right-of-way of all portions of the Interstate System consistent with national standards to be promulgated by the Secretary of Commerce. It directed that the national standards shall provide for:

1. directional and other official signs;
2. signs advertising the sale or lease of property upon which they are located;
3. signs not larger than 500 square inches advertising activities being conducted at a location within twelve miles of such signs, and
4. signs authorized by state law to give information in the specific interest of the traveling public. (See illustration on page 151.)

Section 12 authorized the Secretary of Commerce to enter into agreements with state highway departments to carry out the national policy with respect to the Interstate System within the state. Within the discretion of the Secretary, and consistent with the national policy, the agreements could provide for excluding from advertising control segments of the Interstate System which traverse incorporated municipalities, where use of real property adjacent to the system is subject to municipal regulation, or which traverse other areas where the land use is clearly established by state law as industrial or commercial, or which are built on rights-of-way wholly acquired before July 1, 1956.

An incentive for state implementation of the national policy was provided by authorizing a one-half of 1 percent increase in the federal share of the cost of Interstate projects to which the national policy and agreements apply.

This section also provided that federal funds could be used to pay the federal pro rata share of the costs of acquiring the right to advertise or regulate advertising for the purpose of implementing the section. Federal reimbursement was limited, however, to that portion of such costs which does not exceed 5 percent of the cost of the right-of-way for the project.

The bill was considered by the Senate over a period of four days, March 24–27, 1958, with much of the debate being directed to Section 12, the advertising control provision.

Senator Robert S. Kerr (D-Okla.) led the fight against the control of outdoor advertising and offered an amendment to strike all of Section 12 from the bill. The Kerr amendment was made the pending question, but other amendments were considered before the Kerr amendment was voted upon. Two of these amendments warrant comment.

An amendment by Senator Norris Cotton (R-N.H.) was accepted, which excluded the control of advertising adjacent to any portion of the Interstate System constructed upon right-of-way, any part of the width of which was acquired on or before July 1, 1956. His amendment also deleted the language in the reported bill that permitted the exclusion, by agreement, of segments of the system built on right-of-way wholly acquired before July 1, 1956. The Cotton amendment had the effect of limiting advertising control to areas adjacent to portions of the Interstate System constructed upon new locations.

Senator Francis Case (R-S.D.) offered an amendment, which also was accepted, to strike out the 500 square-inch limitation on the size of signs permitted to be erected and maintained to advertise activities located within twelve miles of such signs.

The crucial vote was on Senator Kerr's amendment to strike all of the advertising control provisions from the bill. This amendment was rejected by a vote of forty-one yeas and forty-seven nays. It is interesting to note that President Johnson insisted that Congress pass a new and highly questionable advertising control bill in 1965, but as a Senator and the majority leader of the Senate in 1958 voted with Senator Kerr to defeat the control of advertising.

After amending the Senate bill (S. 3414), everything after the enacting clause of the House-passed bill (H.R. 9821) to enact the Federal-Aid Highway Act of 1958 was stricken and the text of the Senate bill as amended was substituted in lieu thereof. This House bill, as amended by the Senate, then went to a committee of conference of the House and Senate to resolve the differences between the two versions of the bill.

The House Committee on Public Works had held no hearings on the control of advertising, and the House had not considered the matter when it passed the bill. The House conferees accepted the advertising control provisions as passed by the Senate without any change.

The conference report (H.R. Report No. 1591, 85th Congress, 2d Session) was debated in the House on April 3, 1958. Representative

J. Harry McGregor (R-Ohio) moved to recommit the conference report to the committee of conference, so as to permit the House Committee to hold hearings on advertising control and to consider the subject. The motion failed by a vote of 109 yeas and 222 nays. The conference report was agreed to by both the House and the Senate, and the Federal-Aid Highway Act of 1958 (P.L. 85-381) was approved by President Eisenhower on April 16, 1958. Thus, the first federal law to regulate outdoor advertising came into being. The advertising control provisions were later codified as Section 131 of Title 23, United States Code.

FEDERAL-AID HIGHWAY ACT OF 1959

In September of 1959, the Senate Committee on Public Works approved an amendment by Senator Kerr to the House-passed Federal-Aid Highway Act of 1959 (H.R. 8678, 86th Congress, 1st Session) pertaining to the control of advertising in commercial and industrial areas. The Kerr amendment struck out the language of the act passed in 1958, which permitted the exclusion of commercial and industrial areas from advertising control if so provided in agreements between the Secretary of Commerce and the state highway departments, and substituted in lieu thereof a mandatory requirement that the agreements not apply to certain commercial and industrial areas adjacent to the Interstate System.

When the bill was considered by the Senate, Senator Neuberger offered an amendment to strike out the Kerr amendment. Senator Neuberger's amendment lost by a vote of thirty-nine yeas and forty-four nays.

Again, President Johnson, then a Senator, voted with Senator Kerr against the control of advertising.

The House, without having held any hearings on advertising control, concurred in the Senate amendment.

APPLICATION OF THE 1958 FEDERAL LAW
AND NATIONAL STANDARDS

The 1958 law, as amended in 1959, was not designed to effectuate advertising control itself but, instead, to encourage and assist the states to control outdoor advertising.

To promote the safety, convenience and enjoyment of public travel and the free flow of interstate commerce and to protect the public investment in the Interstate System, the Congress declared it to be a national policy that "the erection and maintenance of outdoor advertising signs, displays, or devices within 660 feet of the edge of the right-of-way and visible from the main-traveled way of all portions of the Interstate System constructed upon any part of the right-of-way, the entire width of which is acquired subsequent to July 1, 1956, should be regulated consistent with national standards to be prepared and promulgated by the Secretary . . . ."

The law authorized the Secretary to enter into agreements with the state highway departments to carry out the national policy, but provided that such agreements shall not apply to segments of the Interstate System which traverse commercial or industrial zones within the presently existing boundaries (as of September 21, 1959) of incorporated municipalities or other areas where the land use, as of September 21, 1959, was clearly established by state law as industrial or commercial.

Generally speaking, the national policy applied only to those portions of the Interstate System constructed upon completely new right-of-way, outside of commercial or industrial areas.

The law provided for the promulgation of national standards by the Secretary of Commerce, which standards establish the minimum control of advertising to be effected by the states to become eligible for the one-half of 1 percent increase in the federal share of the cost of Interstate highway projects. The national standards were promulgated on November 10, 1958 (23 F.R. 8793, Nov. 13, 1958), and amended on January 12 and March 26, 1960 (25 F.R. 218 and 2575), to accommodate the changes made in the law in 1959.

Time does not permit a detailed discussion of each of the provisions of the 1958 law and the national standards promulgated thereunder. I wish to discuss their major features, for whatever historical value it may be and because the agreements entered into by twenty-five states to carry out this law, now repealed, and its standards, are still recognized for continuation of the one-half of one percent bonus payments.

The 1958 act required that the national standards include provisions permitting four specified classes of signs, and no others, in areas adjacent to controlled portions of the Interstate System. These four classes of signs were described in general terms in the national standards.

> Class 1: *Official signs*—Directional or other official signs or notices erected and maintained by public officers or agencies pursuant to and in accordance with direction or authorization contained in state or federal law, for the purpose of carrying out an official duty or responsibility. (See page 153.)

The standards contained no specific provisions with respect to Class 1 signs. It was considered appropriate for each state legislature to determine the type, number and location of official signs. These signs ordinarily would not include official traffic signs, which usually are placed within the right-of-way. The federal law applied only to areas adjacent to the right-of-way.

> Class 2: *On-premise signs*—Signs not prohibited by state law which advertise the sale or lease of, or activities being conducted upon, the real property where the signs are located.

On-premise signs advertising the sale or lease of property were subject to a maximum size limitation of 150 square feet. The standards permitted only one such sign that could be viewed by traffic moving in any one direction on an Interstate highway. (See page 155.)

Signs advertising activities being conducted on the premises were not subject to limitations as to number or size, except for signs located more than fifty feet from the advertised activity. These latter signs were limited in size to 150 square feet, and there could be only one such sign viewed by traffic moving in any one direction on any one Interstate highway.

Class 3: *Signs within 12 miles of advertised activities*—Signs not prohibited by state law which advertise activities being conducted within 12 air miles of such signs.

Class 3 Signs. Signs May Have To Be Relocated, If Not Within 12 Air Miles of the Advertised Activity

Picture Credit: *U. S. Bureau of Public Roads*

The standards limited the size of this class of signs to 150 square feet. Only one sign advertising a single enterprise and visible to traffic moving in any one direction on any one Interstate highway was permitted.

Class 4: *Signs in the specific interest of the traveling public*—Signs authorized to be erected or maintained by state law which are designed to give information in the specific interest of the traveling public; such as, information about public places operated by federal, state, or local governments, natural phenomena, historical sites, areas of natural scenic beauty or naturally suited for outdoor recreation, and places for camping, lodging, eating, and vehicle service and repair.

Class 4 Signs. These Are Signs in the Specific Interest of the Traveller

Picture Credit: *U. S. Bureau of Public Roads*

There was no mileage limitation as to the distance between a Class 4 sign and the advertised activity. These signs were also limited in size to 150 square feet, and only one sign advertising a single enterprise or place and visible to traffic moving in any one direction on any one Interstate highway was permitted.

The standards contained other provisions with respect to the location, spacing and frequency of Class 3 and Class 4 signs.

No signs visible to traffic on an Interstate highway approaching an exit roadway were permitted in controlled areas for a distance of two miles in advance of the intersection of the Interstate highway and the exit roadway. This was to eliminate the competition of advertising signs with official traffic signs within a critical area of driver decision. Six such signs were permitted in controlled areas not less than two or more than five miles in advance of the intersection of an exit roadway. In controlled areas more than five miles in advance of the intersection of an exit roadway, an average of one such sign per mile was permitted.

No signs visible to Interstate highway traffic which is approaching or has passed an entrance roadway were permitted in controlled areas for 1,000 feet beyond the intersection of the entrance roadway and the Interstate highway.

Subject to the foregoing provisions, not more than two Class 3 or 4 signs were permitted within any mile distance measured from any point, and all such signs had to be at least 1,000 feet apart. (See page 174.)

Class 2 (on-premise) signs and Class 3 and 4 (off-premise) signs were subject to other provisions of the standards pertaining to obstruction of view, lighting, animation, movement and resemblance to official traffic signs or signals.

The standards also provided for the establishment of informational sites, where Class 3 and 4 signs, not more than twelve square feet in size, could be displayed upon panels.

No state was obligated to control outdoor advertising under the 1958 law, and no penalty was imposed for failure to do so. The method of control was left up to each individual state. Some states effected control by exercise of police power, through regulation and zoning. Some accomplished the desired results by the purchase or condemnation of advertising rights. Others utilized a combination of police power and the power of eminent domain.

Any state that acquired advertising rights by purchase or condemnation was entitled to reimbursement of the federal share, ordinarily 90 percent, of the cost of such acquisition not exceeding 5 percent of the costs of right-of-way for the project.

The 1958 act, as amended, allowed the states until June 30, 1965, to enter into advertising control agreements with the Secretary so as to become eligible for payment of the additional one-half of 1 percent federal share of the cost of Interstate highway construction projects. By June 30, 1965, twenty-five states had entered into such agreements. A total of $1,936,153 have been paid to fourteen states pursuant to these agreements.

The Highway Beautification Act of 1965 (P.L. 89-285), which repealed the 1958 act by amending Section 131 of Title 23, United States Code, provides that any state which entered into an agreement with the Secretary under the prior law shall be entitled to receive the bonus payments set forth in the agreement if the state maintains the control required under the agreement or the control required by the 1965 act, whichever control is stricter. It is possible for all twenty-five of the states to receive bonus payments until completion of construction of the Interstate System, which probably will not be accomplished before 1975.

In his message to Congress on the natural beauty of our country on February 8, 1965 (H. Doc. No. 78, 89th Congress, 1st Session), President Johnson pointed out that the authority for states to enter into agreements with the Secretary for the control of outdoor advertising expire on June 30, 1965. He stated that the provisions of the program then existing had not been effective in achieving the desired goal and that he would recommend legislation to insure effective control of billboards along our highways. The President also said that he intended to call a White House Conference on Natural Beauty to meet in mid-May of 1965, under the chairmanship of Mr. Laurance Rockefeller.

The White House Conference, made up of fifteen eight-man panels, was held on May 24 and 25, 1965. The Panel on Roadside Control, chaired by Mr. Howard S. Ives, Connecticut State Highway Commissioner, considered the control of outdoor advertising, along with other subjects. Mr. Philip Tocker, one of the speakers at this symposium, was a member of that panel.

According to the published proceedings of the conference, a vote was taken at a meeting of the Panel on Roadside Control following the panel session, and all panelists present, with one exception, voted to recommend that no off-premise advertising be permitted in any areas adjacent to the primary system and the Interstate System. Two panelists who were unable to be present asked that the report show that they would have voted to permit off-premise advertising in certain commercial and industrial areas.

The day after the close of the conference, President Johnson sent to the Congress a message on highway beautification (H. Doc. No. 191, 89th Congress, 1st Session) wherein, among other things, he recommended new legislation for the control of outdoor advertising.

HIGHWAY BEAUTIFICATION ACT OF 1965

Advertising control legislation recommended by President Johnson was introduced in the House on May 26, 1965, by Representative George H. Fallon (D-Md.), chairman of the Committee on Public Works (H.R. 8489), and by Representative John C. Kluczynski (D-Ill.), chairman of the Subcommittee on Roads of the Committee on Public Works (H.R. 8490). On June 3, 1965, Senator Jennings Randolph (D-W.Va.), chairman of the Senate Committee on Public Works, introduced identical legislation as Title I of S. 2084.

The President's recommended legislation would revise Section 131 of Title 23, United States Code, by eliminating all of the provisions of the act passed in 1958, as amended, and substituting new language to accomplish the following:

1. Require the states to control outdoor advertising, as provided in the bill, along the Interstate System and the federal-aid primary system, within 1,000 feet of the nearest edge of the pavement.

2. No federal-aid highway funds would be apportioned on or after January 1, 1968, to any state which has not made provision to control advertising as required by the bill, thereby imposing a 100 percent penalty.

3. All off-premise advertising signs would be prohibited, except (a) within areas zoned industrial or commercial under authority of state law and (b) within areas not zoned under authority of state law but which are used predominantly for industrial or commercial activities, as determined in accordance with national standards to be established by the Secretary of Commerce.

4. The only signs that would be permitted outside of commercial or industrial areas are (a) directional and other official signs required or authorized by law and (b) on-premise signs advertising the sale or lease of, or activities being conducted upon, the real property where the signs are located. All of these signs would have to conform to national standards to be promulgated by the Secretary.
5. Nonconforming signs would not be required to be removed until July 1, 1970.
6. Federal-aid highway funds could be used to pay the federal pro rata share of the costs of controlling advertising by purchase or condemnation but only if the state is unable to secure the required control under its police power.
7. The state highway departments would be authorized to maintain maps and to permit informational directories and advertising pamphlets to be made available at safety rest areas and, subject to the approval of the Secretary, to establish information centers at safety rest areas.
8. The rights of states to receive the one-half of 1 percent bonus payments in accordance with agreements entered into under the 1958 act would be preserved, without being conditioned upon compliance with the proposed legislation.

The House Subcommittee on Roads held hearings on the President's proposal on July 20, 21, and 22, 1965. These hearings disclosed the existence of many problems and unanswered questions and demonstrated rather conclusively that the legislation should be substantially revised to provide for a workable program. It was the understanding of the Committee that, because of the great amount of revision needed and the heavy work load of the Committee, the Committee and its staff would study the bills but final action would not be taken until early in 1966.

Despite this understanding and the good and valid reasons supporting it, a sudden decision was made to reopen the hearings, and hearings were held on September 3 and 7, 1965.

The Subcommittee on Roads held executive sessions on the legislation on September 13, 14, 15, and 16, 1965. On two of these dates, sessions were held both during the day and at night. This was done in spite of the fact that the Senate was then considering the highway beautification bill. The minority members of the House Committee on Public Works insisted that the matter was not so urgent that it could not wait until the Senate completed action and the Committee had before it the bill to be passed by the Senate. On Friday, September 17, an executive session of the Committee was scheduled, but at the last minute it was postponed to await receipt of the Senate-passed bill.

The full Committee met in executive sessions on September 20 and 21 and marked up the Senate-passed bill (S. 2084), making only minor changes in the advertising control provisions. At the close of the September 21 meeting, a majority of the Committee agreed to report out the bill, and it was directed that the committee report on the bill be filed with the House by midnight of the next day, which was done.

Seven members of the Committee filed minority views with the committee report (H.R. Report 1084, 89th Congress, 1st Session) opposing enactment of the bill as reported. The minority views set forth in detail many of the inadequate and objectionable features of the legislation, which are summarized at the beginning of the views, as follows:

> We support the concept of beautifying areas adjacent to highways, but we are opposed to the enactment of this bill in its present form, for three basic reasons:

1. It is not the product of careful, independent congressional deliberation. Instead, it is a poorly thought out proposal which was brutally forced upon the Committee on Public Works by spokesmen for the administration who wielded the power and influence of the White House, to an extent which we have never before seen, to make certain that the bill be reported, and reported *now*, regardless of the consequences.

2. The bill is replete with unworkable, unwise, and unfair provisions insisted upon by spokesmen for the administration who did not know and probably did not care about the many ramifications and adverse impacts of such provisions.

3. The bill will unjustly penalize states which, in good faith, may attempt to control outdoor advertising and junkyards under the bill, but are unable to do so within the short time allowed, because of constitutional or other impediments; it will have a destructive impact upon small businesses, such as motels, hotels, restaurants, service stations, and the like, which depend upon patronage by the motoring public for survival and it will deprive the motoring public of needed travel information.

The day before the bill was considered on the floor of the Senate, the administration sent to the Senate several amendments to the committee-reported bill. Some of these amendments, which were adopted by the Senate and retained by a majority of the House Committee at the insistence of the administration, contributed to the opposition to the bill by the members who filed the minority views.

The "White House arm twisting" employed to force upon the Congress specific language contained in the bill, and the unworkable and unwise provisions of the law resulting therefrom, are discussed in the minority views. It is appropriate to observe that in 1965 President Johnson was far more successful in passing the law that he wanted for the control of outdoor advertising than he was, as a Senator, seven years earlier in trying to defeat the first advertising control law.

The heavy hand of the White House remained much in evidence when the bill was considered on the floor of the House on October 7, 1965. Amendment after amendment to improve the bill and make it more workable was rejected by a partisan majority.

Of the few amendments agreed to by the House, one by Representative J. Russell Tuten (D-Ga.) has been particularly important in the subsequent interpretation and administration of the law. His amendment added a requirement for consistency with customary usage, in reference to the size, lighting and spacing of signs in commercial and industrial areas. It also provided that the states shall have full authority to zone areas for commercial or industrial purposes under their laws and that such actions of the states will be accepted for purposes of the Highway Beautification Act.

The Senate concurred in the few amendments made by the House, and President Johnson signed the Highway Beautification Act of 1965 on October 22, 1965.

Title I of the Act amended Section 131 of Title 23, United States Code. I will briefly review the major provisions of the new law.

1. Congress declared that the erection and maintenance of outdoor advertising in areas adjacent to both the Interstate System and the federal-aid primary system should be controlled to protect the public investment in the highway, to promote the safety and recreational value of public travel, and to preserve natural beauty.

Questions have been raised as to whether the remaining provisions of the statute, and the manner in which it is being administered by the Department of Transportation, are consistent with these objectives.

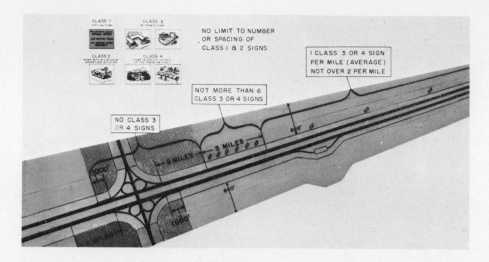

This Drawing Shows the Spacing of Class 3 and 4 Signs on the Interstate Highways under the Federal-Aid Act of 1958 and 1959

Picture Credit: *U. S. Bureau of Public Roads*

2. The states are required to make provision by January 1, 1968, for the effective control of outdoor advertising within 660 feet of the edge of the right-of-way and visible from the main traveled way of all Interstate and federal-aid primary highways.

The 1965 act applies to the entire 41,000 miles of the Interstate System and the 227,898 miles of the primary system; whereas, the prior law applied only to those portions of the Interstate System which are outside of commercial and industrial areas and constructed upon new locations.

3. Effective control means that after January 1, 1968, all off-premise signs are prohibited, except directional and other official signs and notices.

The law provides that any sign lawfully in existence along the Interstate or primary systems on September 1, 1965, which does not conform to Section 131 shall not be required to be removed until July 1, 1970, and that any other sign lawfully erected shall not be required to be removed until the end of the fifth year after it becomes nonconforming to Section 131. I predict that this moratorium provision will be subject to varying interpretations and will be the source of many problems. The administration has already interpreted it to apply differently to signs in commercial or industrial areas than in other areas.

Directional and other official signs and notices, which include those pertaining to natural wonders, scenic and historical attractions that are required or authorized by law, must conform to national standards promulgated by the Secretary of Transportation concerning lighting, size, number, spacing and such other provision as may be prescribed.

4. On-premise signs advertising the sale or lease of, or activities conducted upon, the real property upon which such signs are located are permitted under the act without any regulation or control.

In spite of the fact that on-premise signs are frequently more objectionable than off-premise signs, the act exempts them from regulation either by national standards or by agreements between the Secretary and the states.

5. Separate and apart from "effective control," certain off-premise advertising signs may be erected and maintained in commercial or industrial areas pursuant to agreements between the Secretary and the several states.

The size, lighting and spacing of such signs must be consistent with customary use to be determined by agreements between the Secretary and the several states. The customary use may vary from state to state, and possibly as between areas within a single state.

Such signs may be erected and maintained only in areas which are zoned commercial or industrial under authority of state law, which zoning action will be accepted by the Secretary, or in unzoned commercial or industrial areas as may be determined by agreement between the Secretary and a state.

This provision of the act has been the source of greatest difficulty in both the legislative and administrative process. Its application will determine in a large measure the ultimate success or failure of the advertising control program as well as its cost.

6. Federal-aid highway funds apportioned on or after January 1, 1968, to any state which the Secretary determines has not made provision for effective control of advertising shall be reduced by amounts equal to 10 percent of that which would otherwise be apportioned to such state, unless the Secretary determines that suspension of application of this provision to such state is in the public interest. Any funds withheld from a state shall be reapportioned to the other states.

The Secretary has announced that he has no expectation of imposing any penalties during the year 1968.

7. The Secretary is required, in consultation with the states, to provide within the right-of-way of the Interstate system for areas at appropriate distances from interchanges where signs, displays, and devices giving specific information in the interest of the traveling public may be erected and maintained.

This provision was designed to provide a substitute means of informing the traveling public of facilities for eating, lodging, and vehicle service when off-premise advertising is eliminated from noncommercial and nonindustrial areas adjacent to the Interstate System. Signs erected under this provision must conform to national standards promulgated by the Secretary.

To the extent that signs are used for this purpose, it merely transfers advertising from private property to the public highway right-of-way. This method of providing information about needed facilities appears to be adequate from the viewpoint of both the motorists and the operators of such facilities. Furthermore, the cure may be worse than the ailment, for it creates many new problems and dangers, not the least of which is the possibility of favoritism in the allocation of the limited advertising space available.

Ths provision applies to the Interstate System only. Travelers on the vast rural mileage of the primary system will have no source of sign information of essential facilities.

8. The states are required by the act to pay just compensation to sign owners and to owners of real property on which signs are located upon the removal of signs (a) lawfully in existence on the date of enactment of the act (October 22, 1965), (b) those lawfully on any highway made a part of the Interstate or primary system on or after October 22, 1965, and before January 1, 1968, and (c) those lawfully erected after January 1, 1968. Federal funds will pay 75 percent of such compensation.

The Attorney General of the United States has ruled that this provision of law requires every state to provide just compensation as a condition of receiving the whole amount of federal-aid highway funds apportioned to it on or after January 1, 1968, and that there is no basis for concluding that this requirement is unconstitutional. Even if a state, under its laws and constitution, could require the removal of such signs by exercise of its police power without payment of compensation, the federal law requires that compensation be paid.

However, compensation is not required to be paid for the removal of all lawfully erected signs. For example, compensation is not required to be paid for the removal of any sign lawfully erected after October 22, 1965, and before January 1, 1968, along any highway that was made a part of the Interstate or primary system prior to October 22, 1965, and has continued to remain on such system. If the state doesn't pay compensation in such instance, the owner of the sign and the owner of the land on which the sign is located will not be fairly treated in relationship to other owners who do receive compensation. If the state should pay compensation in such instance, then the state will not be fairly treated for the federal government will not reimburse the state for any part of the payment.

9. Provision is made for the continuation of bonus payments to states which entered into agreements to control advertising under the 1958 act, as amended, provided they continue to control advertising under the terms of their agreements or under the 1965 act, whichever is stricter.

10. The act and national standards apply to public lands of the United States; use of maps, informational directories and advertising pamphlets at safety rest areas is authorized; and a procedure is established whereby any state that is dissatisfied with certain determinations of the Secretary has the right of a hearing and the right to appeal the Secretary's order to the courts.

The 1965 act is replete with poorly drafted, unworkable, unwise and unfair provisions too numerous to discuss at this time. Many of the deficiencies in the law have been demonstrated by the proposed standards and criteria prepared by the Secretary for administration of the act, and they will become greater obstacles to success of the program as it continues.

IMPLEMENTATION OF THE 1965 ACT

The Secretary has prepared and published three different versions of proposed standards and criteria for administering the advertising control provisions of the Highway Beautification Act of 1965. They were released on January 28, 1966, July 1, 1966, and January 16, 1967. All three versions have been unacceptable to the Congress.

The last of the proposed standards and criteria were submitted to the Congress as a part of the 1967 Highway Beautification Program Report (H.R. Doc. No. 6, 90th Congress, 1st Session). Extensive hearings were held in April and May of 1967 by the House Subcommittee on Roads on the entire highway beautification program, including this report and legislation requested by the administration to authorize the appropriation of funds for fiscal years 1968 and 1969 to finance the program.

It would take hours to discuss all of the problem areas, but their magnitude is demonstrated by the fact that of the 1,100,020 off-premise advertising signs in existence along the Interstate and primary systems, the administration proposed to remove 1,016,792. Of this number, the law itself would require the removal of all 839,361 off-premise signs outside of commercial or industrial areas, without any adequate alternative means of providing the traveling public with needed information. In 1967, the administration estimated that the cost of removing these signs would be $558,610,000. Other witnesses, including officials of many states, testified that the cost would be far in excess of the administration's estimate. In 1965, when the administration was urging passage of the bill, it advised the Congress that the maximum federal cost for advertising control would be $180,000,000.

The situation is well summed up by a statement made by Representative John C. Kluczynski (D-Ill.), chairman of the House Subcommittee on

Roads, at the last day of the hearings on May 3, 1967, which is quoted in part as follows:

> . . . Had we had hearings in 1965 like we have had right now and the discussion, I believe we would have come up with a better act and better legislation. These hearings have clearly expressed the dissatisfaction of virtually all groups with the program as it is presently working. As a practical matter it really makes no difference whether the effective law is at fault or its administration is at fault. If the program is to be preserved and go forward to any measure of accomplishment, changes evidently will have to be made. There seems little hope of continued congressional approval for the program or the funds needed for it unless those changes are made. And, gentlemen, I know better than anybody in Congress because the state delegations come to me as chairman of this Subcommittee on Roads and I mean the full state delegations—not only one or two members of Congress. They were the ones who asked me to hold these hearings and, as you know, we have heard over 70 witnesses . . . I believe we enacted a can of worms. Believe me when I say that. I am going to try to untangle that. . . .
>
> Gentlemen, believe me when I say this. We have our work cut out for us, and I would hope we can sit down and write up a bill that will be satisfactory to all of us.

PRESENT STATUS OF THE HIGHWAY BEAUTIFICATION PROGRAM

At the present time the highway beautification program is at a standstill as far as undertaking new projects is concerned. We are now at the midpoint of fiscal year 1968, and the last funds authorized for the program were for fiscal year 1967, except for the federal government's administrative expenses.

An Illustration of an Informational Site, Proposed in the Standards

Picture Credit: *U. S. Bureau of Public Roads*

Secretary of Transportation Alan S. Boyd has announced that he has no expectation of imposing any penalties against the states during the year 1968 and for some time into 1969 in order that the states may have adequate time to enact legislation and negotiate agreements to implement the act.

The Senate passed a bill (S. 1467, 90th Congress, 1st Session) on August 28, 1967, to authorize the appropriation of five million dollars for fiscal year 1968 to finance the outdoor advertising control program. A majority of the members of the House Committee on Public Works approved the bill, and it was reported to the House on September 27, 1967 (H.R. Report No. 713, 90th Congress, 1st Session). The committee report discusses some of the shortcomings in the program, and fourteen members of the Committee signed minority views filed with the report in opposition to the bill. No action is expected to be taken on the bill by the House this year.

It is hoped that the House Subcommittee on Roads will hold further hearings on this matter next year and rewrite the law so as to make it more realistic and workable.

VIII. CRITICISM OF HIGHWAY SIGNS AND ADVERTISEMENTS

Patrick Horsbrugh

The expression of criticism is not only an act of judgment, it is also the art of demonstrating comparative values. In the following critical observations, I shall attempt to show certain grievous shortcomings in the legally accepted system of general outdoor advertising which allegedly offend those of us who may be visually "high strung."

Professor John W. Houck has stated:

> When two legitimate societal interests clash, an accommodation must be worked out. If this is not possible, society may have to go without one or both of the interests. I believe that America is big enough, varied enough, and wise enough to satisfy both the claims of highway beautification and outdoor advertising.

My colleague, Professor Houck, seems to imply that both highways and outdoor advertising shall remain a permanent feature of the inhabited scene, and that some rational basis to ensure this perpetual coexistence must be established. This premise implies also that policies of land uses and responsibilities shall remain as hitherto and that the public temperament will continue to accept these visual "affronts" indefinitely, as part of the absolute right of the owner to use or to permit uses of his land as suits his financial aspirations best.

Notwithstanding the powerful arguments based upon economic urgencies, commercial convenience and social significance, which suggest that these features of the highway are a permanent reality, I contend that the highway sign is a temporary incident upon the cultivated landscape, and that the near future will witness its gradual decay and disappearance. I question any implications of permanence and continued social acceptance of billboards. I do this, first, upon the strength of the indisputable evidence of the waywardness of fashion—people do change their minds as to what they find acceptable. And second, I doubt that highways will continue to provide the necessary conditions for the transmission of casual advertising according to the present formula of the billboard. Intellectual opinion and popular fancy continue to change for the sake of change as well as for practical reasons, and it is upon this simple factor of fashion, and changes in the conditions of highways, that I shall try to convince you that criticisms of a basically offensive system favoring specialized interests at the expense of the public are sound in respect to changes in popular aesthetic preferences and temperamental tolerances.

IMPERMANENCE OF THE PRESENT ACCEPTANCE OF HIGHWAY SIGNS

Valid criticism of matters of mechanical and commercial significance must include a reference to time and to endurance. Upon the establishment of these dimensions of the calendar rests not only the rhythms of fashionable change but those other factors of effort to be spent and the economic benefit supposedly gained. Even though the financial investments made on obviously temporary short-term conditions may be steadily increasing, it seems to be clear that the pace of life is now such that the duration of fashions and social acceptance is becoming ever shorter. A point may soon be reached where the measure of this rapidity of change becomes so short that financial policies and advertising investments are revised in favor of long-range returns, where the threatening edge of impermanence is less abrasive.

In human affairs there are distinct cycles of preference, instinctive and stimulated, which assure change and which are still only vaguely understood, though much researched. For half a century now it has been the commercial habit to advertise along the roadside, both on-premise and off-premise, and the quantity of signs has steadily increased until the physical density and visual confusion has reached a point where opinions, both cultivated and uninformed, are registering both dislike and bewilderment. In evidence, I refer the reader to 1958 federal act offering a bonus to the states if they limit outdoor advertising on the Interstate System. And, of course, if legislation can be considered as an indicator of public opinion, I cite the passage of the Highway Beautification Act of 1965 with its far-reaching regulation of outdoor advertising along the federal Interstate and primary highway systems.

The pendulum of national preference is swinging from the present toleration, which leads to visual indigestion and abhorrence, to a desire to regulate the growth of roadside signs, which are becoming a public nuisance and a national shame. This tolerance of outdoor advertising demonstrates the extent to which a publicly financed facility, the highway, is dominated by specialized interests—the advertiser, the landowner, the billboard owner, the roadside businessman—whose interests are mostly irrelevant to the act of movement, the enjoyment of travel, the character of the community and the quality of the landscape. What of the interest of the travelers, the general users and taxpayers in a visual atmosphere along their highways of openness and beauty, which some of us consider to be a new basic democratic right? May I quote from President Kennedy's speech delivered at Amherst College, Massachusetts, in October, 1963:

> I look forward to an America which will not be afraid of grace and beauty, which will protect the beauty of our natural environment, which will preserve the great old American houses and squares and parks of our national past, and which will build handsome and balanced cities for our future.

To avoid misunderstanding, I want to make clear that I do not challenge the need to advertise in our complex and rich economy. As a planner I wish to encourage attempts to simplify our economic complexity, in the belief that much of the present confusion is willful and irrelevant to our general well-being, especially in respect to the visual effects of outdoor advertising, the very instrument which, if effectively used, can bring simplification of action and of economy.

I base my critical analysis, instead, upon three factors: first, the national character of boastfulness and the international and national ramifications of this particular system of visually boastful advertising; second, that there exists a dual responsibility on the part of the outdoor advertising medium to examine the quality of the merchandise advertised and to judge the appropriateness of the market area wherein the advertisement is exposed. I will suggest that both these circumstances are really one morality. Third, I will propose a *principle of relevance* to place and purpose, which may give us a measure of critical and legal assessment as to the placing of highway advertising. I believe that this assessment can lead to the necessary restraints of outdoor advertising that are in the public interest.

"THE FOREIGN INFLUENCE" ON AMERICAN TOURISTS

As an Englishman, may I give some personal observations about what I have found you like and dislike in foreign countries. When overseas I have noted two typically American opinions which arise from the American desire and ability to travel freely abroad. There are always expressions of visual and psychological relief occasioned by the absence of outdoor advertising which is enjoyed in such countries as Switzerland and Denmark. In the latter country no moving signs nor illuminated

Advertising at Its Strongest
Picture Credit: *Signs of Our Time*

animations are permitted. In countries where outdoor advertising is permitted without control of placement, there are complaints that the scene is too similar to that at home and that the expected individuality of place is submerged by the introduction of the familiar blaze of advertising obliterating much of the original charm and variety.

Since the use of similar materials and constructional systems is tending to make the architecture of once different cities increasingly alike, the human spirit is already stirring toward the appreciation of regional distinctions and features of cultural difference. For example, (to allude to American attempts to attract tourists) I refer to the published advertising material declaring the virtues of each state in the union, none of which boast of the quantity of billboards accumulated, nor applaud the use of this form of commercial enterprise as a measure of their economic strength. Indeed, I have never seen billboards shown in these carefully selected illustrations of the scenes they choose to attract attention.

The postwar international race to ape American advertising standards abroad may be found to be very short-lived and to be replaced by a revengeful attitude on the part of those who have found no nourishment in such tinsel, whose higher aesthetic sensitivities forbid indiscriminate advertising and whose commercial restraint has brought a renown which could not be achieved by any process of advertising. (Denmark might be an example.) Such examples demonstrate very clearly that there are other preferences to be served, such as preferences for unhindered vision, which are currently denied by the general permissiveness that prevails here. This foreign influence of a billboard-free scene may be contagious. The prospects of an anti-advertising sentiment arising in these United States, deliberately dressed and used for practical political purposes by one or both political parties, is a positive possibility which I commend to your consideration. At a time when Americans are obliged to face increasing restrictions upon personal liberty in the interest of more equitable accommodation and official planning, the matter of continuing license for specialized commercial interests must inevitably be challenged.

I certainly hope it is not necessary to answer the argument that without outdoor advertising America's economic bonanza would collapse or diminish. These examples of advertisement-free highways by countries of the highest cultural attainment and sophisticated social development show clearly that such advertising systems are not in the least necessary for general economic progress. Other media are available which do not impose upon the visual sensitivities or infringe the pleasant prospects with irritating interruptions.

THE COSTS OF OUTDOOR ADVERTISING BOASTFULNESS

Since advertising has become the linchpin of American enterprise and influence, it can also become the signal of popular disenchantment, especially where international relationships are concerned.

Have you considered, for instance, these innocent commercial appeals as braggardly expressions, becoming unwittingly an instrument of insidious influences at home and of anti-American propaganda abroad at this most difficult moment in the nation's history when uncertainties in foreign policies and military actions are accompanied by unprecedented urban and social unrest? It may seem farfetched to consider this apparently domestic issue—highway beautification and outdoor advertising—in international terms. But I would be remiss if I did not warn you of the effects of highway advertising upon your friends abroad who are hard-pressed to defend this American custom. Certainly there are those who find this feature of the American scene a convenient instrument with which to deride the principles and purposes of this country.

This simple issue of boastfulness is a painful criticism to which you are perhaps most vulnerable, and the billboard, in my opinion, is the supreme symbol of this national frailty. This "visual roadside uproar" proclaims the truth of those popular foreign jests about loud-mouthed Americans. The bombast is beyond dispute. It is impossible to deny. These blazing declarations of the finest "this" and the best "that" and the "you know what most doctors use" exert an accumulative negative effect no less than the desired commercial appeal.

Outdoor advertising is also a form of propaganda. Both are an exercise in the art of selecting "copy," or message, and picking method of conveyance, media. Both are used to produce an idea, a desire or a motivation which is designed to induce social habits for the benefit of commercial or ideological interests whose objectives are not always evident or laudable, or whose long-term results may become highly objectionable. A ready example was the massive din to promote the use of detergents, but only later was there recognition of the consequent pollution to the lakes and streams, attributable to the chemical persistence of detergents. (Maybe we ought to have a law requiring advertisers to tell the bad things, as well as the good things, and oftentimes the irrelevant things, about their products.) It is high time that the two terms, propaganda and advertising, were juxtaposed and compared. Certainly advertising, like propaganda, seems almost inescapable. It is visible in city and country and it intrudes incongruously at almost every vantage point.

Further, I suggest that this system of unbridled roadside advertising is a major contribution to the uglification of the American landscape, a commercially inspired intellectual and emotional affront. It is an aesthetic degradation that is without parallel, by day or by night, in any place of which I am aware. This plethora of advertising on the highways, urban and rural alike, makes people unduly vulnerable to the deformation of national character, for these wayward trivialities conceal the very real civilizing benefits which this nation has to offer.

These apparently endless miles of beaming billboards with their winking, rippling and flashing signs are a form of visual hypnosis, using every device and design for attracting the eye, arousing interest and occupying the mind. These arcades of blinkers not only restrict the vision but bid fair to confine the mind even though they are offered on the premise of imparting information during vehicular progress (at the expense of attention to the hazards of the highway). Being personally concerned with education and the struggle to broaden the inspiration and responsibilities of those who will succeed us, I resent this needless distraction offered at the roadside and refuse to believe that such a system of flagrant imposition upon personal visual liberty cannot be removed. I plead for a rapid revision of priorities because of the urgent need for national intellectual and psychological improvement, a need to which the advertising business has already shown itself well able to contribute constructively.

It can be argued, of course, that this shifting of favor from one form of advertisement (roadside) to another is against the concept of free enterprise. But in the name of open competition I advocate that we encourage those who can contribute positively to the nation's advancement, simultaneously with that of the product advertised, without the degrading effects of visual disorder along the highways.

PSYCHOLOGICAL REACTIONS OF THE HIGHWAY USER

It is claimed that "America is big enough, varied enough, and wide enough to satisfy both the claims of highway beautification and outdoor advertising," and I want now to turn to those claims. On the basis of visual evidence around us, as distinct from the financial balance sheets, these two requirements would appear to be incompatible.

Speaking as a designer, I offer the definition of beauty (in the context of the highway scene) as that which is natural (of nature), and in human terms that which combines logical choice of material, economically used, to achieve some beneficial result, such as a bridge.

The arguments maintaining that beauty is in the eye of the beholder are spurious, since most eyes are directed by mental motivation, and until that particular influence is made known and acknowledged as a standard of judgment, the catch-phrase remains meaningless.

The basic standards of visual beauty are established by the variety and glory of the American landscape itself. The claim that this beauty should be seen without incidental interruption depends solely upon the aesthetic urge of the individual citizen himself, for if he does not want to look, or does not comprehend what is to be seen, then there is no case to be made against the total concealment of the roadside prospect by billboards.

Speaking as a planner, however, it seems to me that as the urban conditions expand, their monotony increases. As the incidental conglomeration of commercial activities spreads outwards toward the next community, the advertising bewilderment intensifies, in quantity, in diversity and in wondrous ingenuity, and a psychological reaction is naturally engendered in the form of resistance. A mental rejection soon develops, an emotional exhaustion from such continuous stimuli ensues and a seething hostility toward such ceaseless messages of exhortation may arise. Such resentment may be expected to erupt as though the billboards were bars that confine urban society, dividing it from those great prospects that this most splendid continent has to offer. Highway signs hinder the right of the freedom to see, the freedom of the choice of view and the freedom of spiritual refreshment stemming from the sight of the horizon. When freedom is the current and potent battle cry, the innocent advertisement may well come to symbolize dark influences of vested interest control and domination that will provoke disorder rather than win the confidence of the consumer.

While it would be unwarranted to suggest that billboards contributed to the Watts explosion or that the Newark riots resulted from diminished visual distances occasioned by the disposition of outdoor advertising, the psychological effect of such visual confinement must be recognized. The risks of social combustion are greatly heightened by the possibilities of urban improvement which is seemingly unobtainable amid conditions of increasing urban and rural squalor.

DUAL CIVIC RESPONSIBILITIES OF THE OUTDOOR ADVERTISING MEDIUM

The suggested "revolution of expectation" is largely the result of the success of advertising, and in the interests of civil harmony, the aesthetic and physical form of such declarations of commercial enterprise should be revised to promote not only the sale of the commodity offered but also the quality of the place from which the customers may be drawn. The present art of outdoor advertising is entirely monodirectional, concentrating upon sale without regard for the place of selling. I submit that the market place is as important as the material to be marketed and that there is a dual responsibility to be undertaken by the advertising business. If the business accepts some guardianship for the nature and quality of the merchandise, it should, by the same token, take care of the condition of the sites which it freely selects for its operations.

I suggest that the responsibilities for product and for placement of signs are not so dissimilar that one can be fostered and the other degraded.

The price of outdoor advertising must now include the protection of the physical amenities from disruptive influences, and the advertiser should feel some compunction towards the environmental consequences that emerge from the placing of each single sign or from the cultivation of those jungles of conflicting "oh-so-urgent" ideas to distract the driver.

The sheer quantity of signs (visual evidence rather than statistical count) has now broadened the design dimension to include the emotional condition of boredom. While repetition of statement by advertising implies importance, there is also the possibility of boredom induced by familiarity, and boredom is the worst of all the social diseases. The fact that the image upon some billboards keeps changing is incidental. Such changes do not provide entertainment enough to compensate for the effects of reducing the separate identity of most urban areas to a degree of absolute anonymity, which is in sharp contrast to the American urge to travel abroad to see that which is different.

It should be acknowledged that in both outdoor advertising and highway design the American enterprise, private and public, has achieved outstanding results in the past twenty-five years. These achievements have set standards which are the envy of all those whose economic conditions are similar, and it is ironic indeed that it is here in the United States that these "two legitimate societal interests," to quote Professor Houck, should produce this conflict between values, commercial and aesthetic, in general economic conditions that are without precedent in all recorded human history.

Highway engineering in the United States has produced a new kinetic art and aesthetic standard, in accord with the particular nature of the terrain thereby exposed to view. This excellence has won high praise abroad.

Outdoor advertising has also developed in dramatic fashion, but it has not won comparable admiration. Instead, it has become a reference of derogation, a measure illustrating the absence of those sensitivities which allows General de Gaulle to declare, with relish, that "The Americans will commit all the stupidities they can think of, plus some that are beyond imagination." Certainly, the total acreage which is now under the glowering influence of roadway signs by day and by night must be enormous both in urban and in rural areas. The accumulative psychological effect caused by this "visual oppression" must now be reexamined with the utmost care. The reexamination must include a measurement of direct and indirect amenity losses as well as the commercial benefits to the advertiser and the outdoor advertising medium.

Some businessmen are already alert to this problem of amenity loss. For instance, I have noticed that many new factories and office buildings are being located in areas which are somehow free from this particular visual burden that so afflicts the American scene. Businessmen, I suspect, are recognizing the high cost of ugliness. Another example of this awareness can be found in the composition and design of advertising copy. Those automobiles illustrated on the pages of magazines are usually shown in some eloquent environmental setting, before the entrance of a luxury hotel, at the country club, or in some idyllic landscape, even on the seashore. But never, it seems, within sight of the highway signs. Is there something of a conscious judgment by the advertiser in this careful avoidance of showing a vehicle in its most usual surroundings, highway blight?

My criticisms of highway signs go beyond the purely aesthetic considerations of position and design of structure, since the nature of the message can scarcely be divided from the means of display, and I base these objections upon the degree of importance of the information to be imparted to those in transit. The preoccupation of the viewer for whom the message is intended is also important.

There are, I suggest, three categories of urgency: vital information involving directions to the driver requiring decision in the interest of public safety; casual information involving choice, such as service, food and accomodation; and irrelevant distractions having nothing whatsoever to do with the progress of movement, the conditions of travel or the place of display.

By comparison with the standard highway information boards, I have no hesitation in condemning the wayside advertising in general as offering irrelevant information at an inappropriate time. Since most billboards are not conveying information connected with the fulfillment of the journey, their locations are inconsequential to the highway design and are determined only by the visual opportunities offered by curves and topographical formations. They are often scattered in flagrant disregard for views and features of scenic value which the traveler may rightfully expect to enjoy during the hours of daylight. I stress this factor of daylight because the situation at night is obviously very different and deserves to be assessed by other standards.

In using this principle of relevance to place and of purpose—both are founded on the highway user's needs—as a basic requirement of good highway sign location and design, it is difficult to justify the incidental arrangements that presently exist as having any other purpose than that of selfish convenience—and selfishness is no longer a sufficient motive for action in this ever more complicated society.

The conflicting pressures of administration, which involve every aspect of the urban and rural scene, are becoming so intense that we can anticipate a full scale reevaluation of the condition of the land of this nation as is the case in Britain, Holland, etc. Such a review of relative

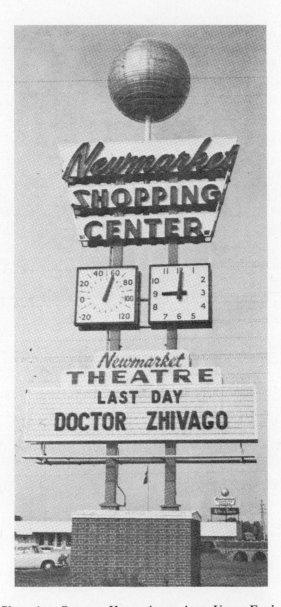

The Shopping Centers Heap Attractions Upon Each Other

values, practical and aesthetic, will be forced upon us by events in the streets, of which we had some foretaste the last few summers. It is inevitable that a revised ethic of responsibilities toward the environs will emerge and will place a far higher value upon the right to see, and to see without hindrance, interruption or distraction caused by the insistence of some gainful-minded concern that has no other obligation than to improve its revenue, no matter at what aesthetic loss.

Is it not extraordinary how we tolerate visual afflictions which we would not permit upon the ear or the nose? In the current literature, it seems that emphasis upon visual freedoms from irrelevant intrusion is being increasingly stressed, and I have not read a single report which advocates the continued distribution of outdoor advertising. The recent report of the Potomac River Basin Task Force, for instance, makes no reference to the accommodation of billboard displays in that region upon the basis of improving local revenues, even though such revenues might be devoted to the cause of scenic improvement in a way similar to that devised by the Italian Autostrade Authority to help reimburse the original construction costs. After repayment for these charges is fulfilled, the billboards are then removed.

As urban conditions decline, so the respect for the natural and the cultivated landscape will increase, and the therapeutic significance of the great outdoors will be recognized as essential to continued urban vitality. In the coming reevaluation of the scene, the erection of billboards, whether scattered across the superbly subtle landscape of Nebraska or rising upon the rooftops of Boston, will be regarded as an ethical transgression imposing unduly upon the public patience, even though no legal breach may be committed.

It will be assumed, by now, that I am implacably opposed to outdoor advertising. But this is not so, for I believe that we can rectify some of the conflicting claims between commercial enterprise and visual freedom (that is, if there are adequate restrictions on highway signs that carry information irrelevant to the highway users' needs).

There is, for instance, the need to design highway signs for commercial activities of genuine interest and immediate relevance that must be accommodated along the highway. There will be signs bearing reference to local facilities, recreational opportunities, restaurants and hotels, and historic features. We are confronted here with the basic matter of selection, legal justification and legislative action, as to what signs will be allowed and encouraged. It will be easier to legislate on a basis of sign purpose than upon aesthetic judgment; it is impossible to maintain legal consistency in regard to the factor of taste or beauty. I suggest, therefore, the principle of relevance to place, to time and to condition as offering better reason for selection and decision. I reiterate that unless some restraints are imposed, there can be no limit to the quantity of wayside signs—in use, out of use or in delapidation.

These principles of place, time and condition have already been resolved in two distinctive features of urban America which have come to great prominence as setting the pace and form of civic design: the supermarket and the airport.

In both these facilities the absence of blatant advertising and the careful display of relevant information has been brought to a high pitch of elegance, even of art. These examples would seem to demonstrate that, notwithstanding the dense concentration of people, and the temptation to take commercial advantage of them in the conventional way, new forms of advertising have been found to be both preferable (aesthetically) and profitable (commercially). Cannot the success of these methods be reapplied for the benefit of the city, the town, the highway and the landscape as a continuous whole?

Of all the businesses which the nation has fostered, there is not one that is more sensitive than that of advertising. It provokes the very will to change, it maintains the rate of change and stimulates the momentum for yet further changes. It would be ironic, indeed, if the advertising business itself were to fall victim to changes in the mood of the public tolerance, not for reasons of what is advertised but because of the method of advertisement. The undoubted skill in the art of advertising in papers, journals, radio and on television, in particular, seems to be wholly absent from the static and repetitious highway signs whose inescapable "aura" may become the basis of their own demise.

NEED FOR GREATER RESEARCH

I would like to make a positive proposal for the investigation of this problem of commercial and aesthetic accommodation. An academic program for detailed study of sign design, placement and effect should be undertaken to explore the nature of the conflicts between commercial interests and aesthetic consequences, with the full sympathy, support and financial backing of the advertising associations.

Many academic institutions are developing new courses for the assessment of environmental conditions with far greater imagination and depth of detail than hitherto. For obvious reasons these programs must make a special effort to deal with those environic influences which have previously been ignored. They should attempt to associate physical conditions with visual values, civic "emotional temperatures" and medical tolerances, in terms which are only theoretical at present. Research of this nature is imperative with respect to the occupation of the shallow seas, the outer spaces and even the more remote parts of the earth, where life is hard and difficult to maintain. How much more important it is that we develop knowledge concerning the adaptability and tolerance of our society, which will be relevant to the art of improving visual conveyance and awareness. By raising the intensity of research on visual environment, it should be possible to design in more imaginative ways outdoor advertising. Thus we can avoid the present degrading conflict of interest and we can develop a logical system of restraints whereby commercial purposes are better served without loss of national renown or scenic quality.

Further, in spite of the gigantic investment, there is no guarantee that the highway will continue indefinitely in its present form and use. As the canal was superseded by the railroad, so in turn the railroad has given place to the highway and the airway. So too will the highway become modified as anti-gravity vehicles (now in the design stages) and vertical flight become economic. It must be recognized that the presently advantageous siting for billboards may not be everlasting. Who would now raise signs along canal banks or beside the railroad tracks?

In the volume *Texas Conference on Our Environment Crisis* I have already identified the need for the systematic study of historic enviria, areas having great historic significance, such as that of Williamsburg, Mesa Verde, and Savannah. The same imperatives apply to the general location and visual response to advertisements, their quantity, arrangement and relevance to place and time, in areas having particular commercial vitality, such as at Aspen, Colorado, and Times Square.

I know of no course of studies that concentrates upon billboard placement and design, or which recognizes commercial advertising as an integral part of the general planning procedure. There are many reasons, aesthetic, economic and legal, why it is necessary that such a course of studies should be developed without delay. The principal motivation of any such course is that of ensuring the civic seemliness that befits a potentially Great Society and a marvelously wealthy commercial community, one which has inherited and seeks to enjoy the most superlative variety of natural scenic beauty ever to have been entrusted to the protection of a single system of popular government. Such a dwindling treasury deserves and cries out for the exercise of better sense and sensitivity.

IX. THE ACCOMMODATION OF HIGHWAY BEAUTIFICATION AND OUTDOOR ADVERTISING

Ross D. Netherton

THE PRINCIPAL PARTIES IN INTEREST

First, who are the parties to this accommodation? And what do they represent as interests in our society and economy?

One of the principal parties, obviously, is the group popularly called the "billboard industry." I refer to it as a group because it is made up of an organized segment, dealing in the service of standardized advertising signs, and an unorganized segment, dealing in advertising which ranges from individual custom-made signboards to series of signs which may or may not have any standardization. The organized segment, some 600 members strong, is represented by the Outdoor Advertising Association of America.[1] The unorganized segment numbers perhaps more than 3,000 business concerns, predominantly in the "small business" category of the economy.[2]

A substantial number of roadside signs are erected by individual advertisers who own and maintain them as part of their business. Some businesses—like the well-known Harold's Club in Reno—actually operate what amounts to a self-sufficient outdoor advertising department within their general business, making, erecting and maintaining their chains of

[1] Phillip Tocker, "Beauty For America," *Proceedings of the White House Conference on Natural Beauty,* May 24–25, 1965 (Washington: GPO, 1965), p. 252.

[2] U.S. Cong., House, "Final Report of the Highway Cost Allocation Study," House Doc. 54, 87th Cong., 1st Sess., Jan. 16, 1961, p. 109.

signboards across the country without recourse to an outdoor advertising sign company.[3] These people are not primarily running a billboard business, however, and so constitute a second major party in interest, the businessman-advertiser group.

In this businessman-advertiser group, three subgroups should be recognized because of their differing objectives and methods of operation. Some operate roadside businesses and are concerned with being able to maintain "on-premise" signs, which are the modern successors to the old painted board mounted on a post at the side of the road or over the door of a store or workshop. Other businesses, not located by the side of the road, are interested in "off-premise" signs, telling people where their store is located and what it sells. Depending on the area which this businessman regards as his market, the intensity of his competition and the amount of his budget he can spend on signs, this man's chain of signs may become quite extensive. A distinction exists between this type of off-premise sign and the signs of a businessman who uses signs not for the purpose of directing people to his door but simply to give his name or trademark maximum public visibility so that by repetition he conditions the public to think of him when the subject of cars or breakfast food or beer or whatever-it-is-he-makes comes up. However, this approach to outdoor advertising is a development of the times and requires that a third subclass of businessman-advertiser be recognized.

Whether this classification of businessmen-advertisers coincides with any other customarily used by economists, I do not know. But I submit that it is a classification that makes sense in evaluating the competing interests involved in the beautification question, and I shall try to show how this works later on.

[3] L. S. Kofoed, "Value of Billboards to Business," Highway Research Circular 23 (Washington: Highway Research Board, April, 1966), p. 27.

Off-Premise and Trademark Signs Are Combined

Moving down the list of parties in interest, there are the owners of road-side land. One segment of this group is interested because they lease roadside land for advertising sites. Its members range from the farm family that rents out space in a pasture for $20 a year to the central city building owner whose rooftop space rents for $1,500[4] a month. The members of this group probably have only one thing in common; that is, in the eyes of the law they have a status as landlords to which property law attaches certain legal consequences.

Moving further into the landowner group, I would recognize another segment composed of those who own land in the vicinity of a site used for outdoor advertising. If, as we have said, the advertising site owners share a common characteristic of status under property law, the same thing is true of these people who are their neighbors. Property law gives them a certain status from which flows certain consequences according to the effects of their neighbor's land use. This has been recognized in economics, sociology and the law for a long, long time. The exact nature and extent of these consequences will, of course, depend on circumstances, but there is no denying that consequences do follow effects.

Mention of the neighbors on adjacent property leads naturally to another group, generally referred to as the highway users or the "traveling public," who, after all, are merely neighbors in the special sense that they occupy for brief periods of passage the strip of land adjacent to the billboard. And it is chiefly to this traveling public that outdoor advertising signs are oriented.

This leads to recognizing another group which is interested in the roadside and which consists of the various public agencies responsible for planning, building, operating and maintaining the public highways. Nowadays we have to recognize that this group of agencies represents

4 "Final Report . . . Cost Allocation Study," note 2 above.

a governmental service and a public interest which is larger than simply an engineering function and viewpoint. This group includes planners (community planners as well as transportation planners), urban renewal programmers, conservationists, recreation and resources developers, groups interested in preservation of historical, architectural or cultural landmarks and others, all of whom share in common the fact that their work is affected by what happens to the highways and the roadsides.

So the problem of working out an accommodation of outdoor advertising and highway beautification involves the interests of nine groups in contemporary society, each of which needs to be understood in terms of our current values before a realistic set of issues can be framed.

PARTIES, POSITIONS AND INTERESTS

Looking in more detail at the interests which each of these groups has in a possible accommodation of billboards and beautification, what can be said of the outdoor advertising industry?

The organized segment described its position on the President's 1965 beautification proposals as follows:

> As far as our medium is concerned, the basic effect of this legislation is, at long last, to recognize that outdoor advertising, as a voice of business and as a business use of land, has a right and a necessity to do business where business is done. In the past this association has consistently opposed legislation that was discriminatory because it failed to recognize that this medium is an integral part of the business and marketing function, and should enjoy the same rights as other businesses. The presently proposed legislation grants that recognition. . . .[5]

[5] Statement of Phillip Tocker, Outdoor Advertising Assn. of America, in U.S. Cong., House, Hearings before Subcommittee on Roads, Committee on Public Works, "Highway Beautification," 89th Cong., 1st Sess., Sept. 7, 1965, p. 421.

More specifically, as to the areas in which the industry felt it had a right to operate, the association indicated that its support was conditioned on the law excepting from federal control all areas zoned by local government for commercial or industrial use and all unzoned areas used predominantly for commercial or industrial activities.

Two other propositions were implicit in this conditional support for a highway beautification program. One was that if signboards were to be removed from areas where they were lawfully located compensation must be paid to the sign owners and landowners. The other was that any such removals should be assigned priorities in relation to the importance they bore to improvement of scenic views.[6] The industry's position was, moreover, a dynamic one, for it contemplated growth of roadside advertising activity as the highway program progressed.

The position of the organized segment of the outdoor advertising industry did not entirely coincide with that of the unorganized segment. Testimony before Congress in 1965 warned that:

> the proposed legislation would improve the competitive position of some of the larger, dominant members of the Outdoor Advertising Association . . . [and] work against a great many smaller sign companies, which, in turn, serve a large part of the many small businesses which cannot afford, and do not need, the national programs offered by the so-called standardized industry.[7]

This was said to be so because the large members of the industry concentrated their operations in cities and their suburbs where zoning patterns tended to be most completely developed. The unorganized small advertising companies, on the other hand, operated mainly in rural

[6] Phillip Tocker, note 1 above, p. 254.
[7] Statement of James Hartzell, Roadside Business Assn., Hearings, note 5 above, p. 144.

areas where zoning remains relatively rare, where chances for establishing the predominance of commercial or industrial use were limited and pressure to recognize scenic areas would be greatest. Basically, therefore, the unorganized segment of the outdoor advertising industry felt that its future could not be assured unless the rural and unzoned areas remained open to them. Unless these areas remained unregulated, or at least left to local zoning bodies to regulate, many small outdoor advertising companies predicted fatal damage to their business.

Small advertisers also expressed in strong terms a desire to correct what they considered an unfair charge, that they were major contributors to roadside ugliness. Citing the fact that many of the objectionable signs were in fact abandoned derelicts whom nobody owned (or maintained),[8] or on-premise signs and displays operated by businessmen-advertisers,[9] these advertising companies have claimed credit for actually improving the areas around their signboards by landscaping and hiding unsightly clutter.[10]

In many respects the interest and position of the unorganized segment of the outdoor advertising industry coincides with that of the roadside business group whom it serves, for the latter has regarded it as essential that its members be able to tell the highway traveler where they are located, what they offer for sale, and how to get there. The Congressional hearings and other recent studies revealed a pattern of advertising strategy for both on-premise and off-premise signs which was influenced by the need to capture business from highways built with limited access. When orienting their signs to expressway travelers, these

[8] Statement of Robert Combs, Hearings, note 5 above, p. 322.
[9] Statement of Richard Robinson, Ohio Valley Advertising Co., U.S. Cong., Senate, Hearings before Subcommittee on Roads, Committee on Public Works, "Highway Beautification and Scenic Road Program," 89th Cong., 1st Sess., Aug. 12, 1965, p. 271.
[10] Ibid., pp. 267–277.

businessmen have sought to design and locate on-premise signs so as to command the view. Large signs, mounted high in the air, have been preferred. Off-premise signs have been designed to give routing directions to guide the motorist off the expressway at the right exit, along the right street or road and into the businessman's parking lot.[11] Naturally, also, off-premise advertisers feel they need sign locations near the exits which are most convenient to their business locations, and numerous enough in advance thereof to win the motorist's patronage in competition with others. And if a businessman is located out of sight of the expressway, he generally feels it necessary to have signs along the local roads and streets to guide the motorist in this unfamiliar area.

The interest of business catering to the motorists' needs—food, lodging, fuel and automotive services—has been responsible for a distinctive pattern of advertising in which an important element is identification of brands of products or services, including acceptance of credit cards. This is the same interest which the so-called "national brands advertisers" have. The latter, however, has a somewhat easier problem since he is not primarily interested in impulse buying. His merchandising objective is satisfied by maximum public exposure of his name and message. His interest, therefore, is in securing visibility along highways having the highest average daily traffic counts.[12] He seeks, and is able to pay for, sites in the densely built-up areas and along rural arterial routes. The roadsides of the Interstate System, comprising 1 percent of

[11] Statement of Rudolph Johnson, International Assn. of Holiday Inns, Hearings, note 9 above, pp. 228–235.

[12] W. C. Biven, and A. J. Cooper, III, *Recommendations Regarding Control of Outdoor Advertising on the Interstate Highway System in Georgia* (Ga. Inst. of Tech., Engineering Experiment Sta., 1962), p. 10, have the following observation:

> The outdoor advertising industry sells coverage rather than space. The amount of traffic passing a sign and the number of travelers seeing the display are measures of its value. This being the case, the industry can hardly be indifferent to regulation of billboards on the interstate system with its high volume of traffic.

the nation's highway mileage and carrying 20 percent of the nation's highway traffic, have always been a prime objective of such advertisers, and this interest dictated their early position that control of outdoor advertising along highways should be left to local government.[13]

Comments on the interest of landowners who provide sites for roadside advertising must be quite general because they comprise a group which is numerous—estimated at 250,000 throughout the United States,[14] widely scattered and completely unorganized. A study of estimated costs and impacts of the 1965 Highway Beautification Act, released by the U. S. Department of Commerce in February 1967, described the landowners' situation this way:

> Landowners typically receive between $30 and $50 annually for each sign rented to an outdoor advertising company. Therefore, except for landowners renting . . . a large number of sign sites, the impact on individual landowners will be relatively small. In terms of total economic losses it should be noted that estimated outdoor advertising company losses already include losses to landowners since some part of annual receipts lost would have been paid to sign site owners . . . About 8 to 10 percent of the receipts outdoor advertising companies receive from renting sign space is paid for site rentals . . . If all sign owners paid land rentals equal to those paid by outdoor advertising companies, losses to sign site owners would be considerably higher . . . However, landowners generally receive income only from the larger advertiser-owned signs.[15]

[13] Statement of Harley Markham, Outdoor Advertising Assn. of America, U.S. Cong., Senate, Hearings before Subcommittee on Roads, Committee on Public Works, "Control of Advertising on Interstate Highways," 85th Cong., 1st Sess., Mar. 26, 1957, p. 301.

[14] U.S. Cong., House, "Third Progress Report of the Highway Cost Allocation Study," House Doc. 91, 86th Cong., 1st Sess., Mar. 2, 1959, p. 53.

[15] U.S. Cong., Senate, "1967 Highway Beautification Program," Senate Doc. 6, 90th Cong., 1st Sess., Feb. 2, 1967, p. 28.

Thus, the landowner's interest would seem to be the same as that of the organized outdoor advertising industry and indicate opposition to extension of roadside sign control. Actually, however, it may not be this simple, for in some instances the lack of sign control works against the landowner. Dr. Dorothy Muncy, a planning consultant for industrial property, has observed that

Private industry has been seeking prestige sites fronting on major highways for more than a decade. Industrial management is spending extra millions for architecture and landscaping to build showcase plants on these prominent sites. Industry wants to present an attractive appearance and to be a good neighbor. This is an example of where private investment can contribute to the appearance of the highway and to natural beauty in the community. But this private investment in handsome industrial buildings and in landscaping should be protected against billboards as neighbors.[16]

Others have noted that landowners in commercial and industrial areas where signs would be permitted under most of the recent proposals for highway beautification programs could expect increased rental income under a regulated system, because of the decreased supply of sign sites, and construction of higher quality signs.[17] Dollar estimates of these direct and indirect benefits to such landowners have not been developed, yet they are factors which are bound to influence some landowners as they assess their interest in proposals for billboard control.

Inevitably, some of the mixed feelings of the owners of roadside advertising sites are shared by the wider circle of landowners who comprise the general neighborhood. The effect of this confusion on the pattern of local advertising sign-control ordinances has puzzled even the keenest

[16] *Proceedings, White House Conference,* note 1 above, p. 267.
[17] Study report, note 15 above, p. 28.

Outdoor Advertising Close To, But Not In,
a Residential Area

Picture Credit: *Signs of Our Time*

observers of American zoning.[18] But, clearly, the seventy-five year history of local advertising sign-control battles is evidence of deep-seated concern over something in the American community's scale of values, and a serious attempt should be made to define it.

There is no question, I presume, about the feeling that outdoor advertising should be excluded from predominantly residential areas. Most people would also say that outdoor advertising has no place in areas where they go for recreation—unless they are intentionally seeking the atmosphere of a carnival midway—nor should it be placed where it is offensive to the setting of natural landmarks or historical or cultural sites. The confusion arises over the commercial and industrial areas and the space which presently is uncommitted and which always has seemed to exist in ample supply. However, it is just this point that disturbs some people as they look at their communities. They note that every year a million acres of land are changed from open space to concrete, stone and masonry by man-made projects,[19] and they urge that billboard control be imposed as part of a wide range of response to the entire complex of threats to environmental quality. Thus, they said in hearings on the 1965 highway beautification proposals:

> Scenic, recreational, fish and wildlife resource values, therefore, should all be part of balanced highway planning and design. The very future shape of the American environment is, in large measure, dependent on the decisions that will be made regarding the pending legislation. . . . Highways must reflect, in location and design, increased respect for the natural unity of the landscape.[20]
> . . . we may see a lot of open space now and take it for granted,

[18] R. F. Babcock, *The Zoning Game* (Madison: 1967), pp. 15–16.

[19] Testimony of Mrs. Thomas Waller, Garden Club of America, Hearings, note 9 above, p. 409.

[20] Testimony of Russell Butcher, National Audubon Society, Hearings, note 9 above, p. 262.

and say we can afford billboards. But how about 10, 20, and 50 years from now? Will we be able to see the countryside? . . . we feel we should be able to zone areas or at least have areas left open along our highways because inevitably, eventually, it will not be that way unless we take steps to establish national standards as some of the states have already done within their own borders.[21]

The city housewife driving to the shopping center, the suburban commuter riding the freeway and the family coming home from a vacation may not express their concern in these terms, but they do react to evidence of the lack of amenity in their community. In explaining Hawaii's success in dealing with the problem of clutter, one of its Senators gave credit to a local women's organization in these terms:

Why were the women of the Outdoor Circle so effective? Their only real weapon was public opinion, but they were able to marshal overwhelming support from those who cherished the natural beauty of the islands.

Today the absence of billboards and community opposition to them is a long-accepted tradition and custom.[22]

Hawaiians may exceed other Americans in their zeal for beautification, but at its core every community has a sense of pride in whatever nature has given it and a resentment toward deterioration and unregulated community clutter. Call it "community conscience" or "neighborhood pride," this feeling is a real factor in the politics of local signboard control. It is a recognition that "things don't really have to be this bad" and a gesture toward making amends for not having planned prudently in the past. Possibly, too, it may be evidence of what the British political scientist, Sir Denis Brogan, has called the American trait of "moral impatience"— an obsession, stemming from Puritanism, that vice can and should be

[21] Ibid., p. 266.
[22] Testimony of Sen. Daniel Inouye, Hearings, note 9 above, p. 161.

punished, and then abolished wherever it appears.[23] If this feeling was not an operational factor in American community outlooks, small billboard companies could not point with satisfaction to letters of commendation for their efforts to clean up and landscape signboard sites or their voluntary action of removing signs from districts where they were out of harmony with the surroundings.[24]

Generally, then, I suggest that the position of the landowner group which we refer to as the "neighborhood" or "the general public" is one which seeks to further the amenity or harmony in community appearance. The welter of local signboard control ordinances that reflect this interest mean, at the very least, that when the public thinks about the community in which it lives, it wants some form of regulation and does not believe this should be left to the self-regulation of the advertising industry and their advertisers.

When these neighbors get into their cars and join the group which we call the "traveling public," their interests and viewpoints undergo some changes. These changes are a reflection, in part, of the reason they are traveling—what they expect to see and do—and, in part, of the needs they have as travelers—what they desire in the way of services.

The typical American motorist devotes 60 percent of his highway mileage to local travel, for business, shopping, and the other things that make up his daily routine. The remainder is spent in travel beyond his local community, either for business or pleasure driving, travel to and from recreational areas or in the course of recreational activities

When he is on local streets and roads, the motorist is on familiar ground and tends to look at signs as part of the landscape. To him the most im-

[23] Sir Denis Brogan, "We're Just Naturally Impatient About the War," *Washington Post,* Oct. 22, 1967, Bl, B2.

[24] Statement of Richard Robinson, Hearings, note 9 above, pp. 267–277.

portant signs are the on-premise signs that show him the shop he is looking for, or, if he can never remember the number of the exit he takes to
get off the beltway to get to the doctor's office, he may remember it by reference to landmarks of some sort, perhaps a signboard. This motorist
accepts signboards as part of the urban design, but he would like this to
be good design. He resents it when signs are too numerous, poorly

On-Premise Advertising:
A Familiar Sight for the Motorist

planned and misused—when it looks to him like each sign is fighting with the other signs around it, and its appearance may even be at odds with the appearance of the building on which it stands or those around it.[25] Particularly does the local motorist resent the illuminated razzle-dazzle that characterizes Main Street or Gasoline Alley at night. Except for a momentary thrill over the blaze of light and color, he thinks this is a downright stupid way to arrange things, because it defeats itself as far as getting across any advertising message and makes it almost impossible for him to pick out the traffic light on the corner until he is practically upon it.

In his role as a local traveler, therefore, the motorist's prime interest is in bringing some order out of the chaos of his community's commercial districts and the streets and roads leading to them. So far as he is concerned, the emphasis of such a system of regulation should be on on-premise signs which are suitably designed to be consistent with the architecture of the buildings they advertise, and arranged so that their usefulness to him is not destroyed by competing extraneous structures, such as the rooftop billboard telling him that dogs love "real meat" dog food.

When, on the other hand, this motorist starts across country with his family, he develops a split personality. In this role, he has been the subject of numerous studies aimed at showing what he needs in the way of information, whether billboards provide this information, how much he can read on a sign as he rides past it, how signs can be made so he can read more, whether signs help him stay alert, and so on. The outdoor advertising industry, roadside business, the neighborhood foes of billboards and their allies in the planning, landscaping and architectural professions, all have drawn from this increasing body of data to explain what the highway traveler really needs and wants. A good deal of dis-

[25] California Roadside Council, Inc., *Signs Out of Control* (San Francisco, n.d.), p. 1.

cretion is required to cut through these gratuitous interpretations and get to what the motorist really thinks for himself. And, in this process, it must, unfortunately, be confessed, he does not always appear to be consistent in what he says.

For example, when the University of Akron recently studied the reaction of motorists on two contiguous sections of Interstate Route 90, one of which allowed roadside advertising and one which did not, it reported that over 70 percent thought the commercial advertising should not be allowed at all on the roadsides. And yet nearly half of this group had not noticed the difference between the regulated and unregulated stretches of highway they had just driven past.[26] More revealing and perhaps more consistent data comes from the study of how and when the highway traveler actually uses billboards. For such data, the recent report on the Economic Impact of the Highway Beautification Act, issued by the U. S. Department of Commerce in February, 1967, and compiled from projects carried on by some twenty-two universities and transportation consultants, is a source of prime importance.[27]

From the extensive findings of these studies, it seems clear that motorists on long-distance trips notice and read billboards, although what they remember depends mainly on whether the message deals with something they want to know in connection with their travel. Their needs and interests in this regard are of three general sorts:

Emergency needs—those normally supplied by police, emergency automotive service vehicles, and ambulances.

[26] Described in A. Kuprijanow, S. Rosenzweig, and M. Warskow, *Motorist Needs and Services on Interstate Highways,* prepared for NCHRP, Highway Research Board (Washington, 1967), p. 74.

[27] U.S. Department of Commerce, *Economic Impact of the Highway Beautification Act: Staff Report* (Washington: Bureau of Public Roads, 1967, multilith), pp. 19–143.

Normal motoring needs—fuel, food, lodging, and routine automotive maintenance.

Supplemental needs—including rest areas, information on routings and off-highway services, with a choice of types, brands and prices.

With respect to emergency needs, the highway traveler neither expects nor gets much help from roadside advertising, except perhaps that it may tell him where he can get to a telephone to call for help.

With respect to his normal travel needs of fuel, food and lodging, a substantial number (from 14 to 40 percent) use outdoor advertising in learning of and locating service establishments.[28] Use of outdoor advertising in actually selecting a restaurant or lodging accommodation, however, varies widely (from 5 percent in New Mexico to 61 percent in Maine).[29] Motorists with reliable alternative means of information reported practically no use of signs in this selection process.[30] As to fuel and automotive services, however, almost half of the groups studied used commercial signs in selecting facilities for these services.[31]

Given a choice between a billboard carrying brand names and an official "Fuel-Food-Lodging" sign, most travelers prefer the brand name, although a substantial minority indicated they had no particular difficulty in finding services with present official information signs.[32] When outdoor advertising was lacking, motorists showed familiarity with various

[28] Ibid., p. 122, citing results of studies by Universities of Memphis State, Tennessee, Washington, Wyoming, the Virginia Department of Highways, Amer. Auto. Assn. and Wilbur Smith Assoc.

[29] Ibid., p. 123, citing results of studies by Universities of Arizona, Memphis State, Missouri, New Mexico State, Washington, Wyoming, the California Division of Highways, and Wilbur Smith Assoc.

[30] Ibid., showing that only 1.4% of AAA members selected accommodations through signs.

[31] Ibid., p. 123.

[32] Ibid., pp. 128–129, citing results of studies by Universities of Akron, Memphis State, Missouri, and Natl. Advertising Co. testimony in Senate hearings.

alternative sources of information, including travel guide books, credit card directories, road maps, information centers, other advertising media, and a willingness to stop and ask questions.[33]

With respect to supplemental needs, motorists' attitudes toward roadside signs were dependent, in some degree, on the product advertised, favoring information about highway services over advertising of other products, and, presumably, reacting in accordance with this preference.[34]

In addition to this measurable evidence of the highway traveler's use of and interest in roadside advertising to secure travel-oriented services, there are other considerations that affect his position regarding billboards and highway beautification. He is, above all, typically human. When he travels to get away from the city, he resents finding billboards where he expects scenery, or in places he remembers as open space, or, as at Gettysburg, the atmosphere of historic events. He sees no good reason why some sensible system of regulation cannot be established to deal with the commercial clutter that seems to move in where there is no planning and control.

If he is city-bred, the motorist on a long trip may, even if he is driving for pleasure or change of scene, welcome a signboard as a symbol of something familiar. Thus, in recent Congressional hearings, a motel owner gave the following insight on his customers' feelings as they drove:

> My guests almost invariably say that occasional driving along highways where nothing is visible, other than grass and trees, is desirable. The same guests say that this type of vista is not preferable for day after day driving, such as is done by interstate travelers. Most of these report they wish to know where and what type of

[33] Ibid., p. 129, based on University of Wyoming study.
[34] Ibid., p. 127, citing results of studies by Universities of Akron, Missouri, Wyoming, and Natl. Advertising Co., AAA, and State of West Virginia.

services are available when needed. They also report that they like to see evidence of civilization. Urban dwellers report they like to see evidence of population and urbanization, and feel a sense of insecurity where they have been insulated from notices of service facilities.[35]

Efforts to measure the highway traveler's reaction to roadside advertising will certainly continue[36] and hopefully will succeed in discovering more about this aspect of the interaction between use of the road and use of the roadside. Currently, however, it is possible to see the highway traveler's interest as a composite one, made up of a desire to see the natural and man-made scene along the roadside without what he considers unnecessary commercialism.[37] He is familiar with other advertising media and can be more self-sufficient than either the businessman or advertising industry gives him credit for. He resents clutter in town and in the country at the same time that he relies on signs to locate and select certain services he needs while traveling. His main perversity, which complicates matters for those who wish to speak for him and say what is best for him, is that he is willing to put up patiently with conditions he does not approve of.

The last group of interested parties is comprised of the governmental agencies responsible for the highway system and for planning, managing, developing and conserving the resources of the city and country in which the public interest is affected by the highway system. We ask these agencies to provide as safe, efficient and convenient a highway system as our technology and public funds permit. We ask the highway departments to design and locate these facilities so they will be integrated with what

[35] Statement of Edgar Sims, American Motor Hotel Assn., Hearings, note 5 above, p. 328.

[36] See, for example, papers published in Highway Research Record 182, "Highways and Environmental Quality" (Washington: Highway Research Board, 1967).

[37] Testimony of Washington Roadside Council, Hearings, note 5 above, p. 71, suggesting that the motorist feels keenly that he has a "right to be let alone."

is being done by other agencies working at urban and rural renewal, parks and recreational facilities, conservation, open space, historical preservation, cultural facilities and pollution control. In this broad mandate, one relatively small aspect concerns the accommodation of roadside advertising to highway beautification.

The highway planner sees his interest in the control of roadside advertising partly in terms of functional engineering design and partly in terms of environmental design. The functional design problem involves, among other things, getting the motorist on, off and along the road as safely and expeditiously as possible. This means that roadside features which unnecessarily compete with official traffic control and informational signs for the motorist's attention must be eliminated, or at least reduced to an acceptable level.[38] Given the deliberate practice of roadside businesses to develop in clusters, this creates a safety and traffic efficiency problem.[39]

A good deal of rhetoric and statistical ammunition has been spent on the so-called "safety issue" of billboard control.[40] Much of the evidence is negative and subject to criticism by statisticians. Yet courts and legislatures that have passed on this basis for roadside advertising regulation have been impressed by the simple logic that these signs compete for the driver's attention while he is driving, and as speeds increase such distrac-

[38] C. Goldschmidt, "Windshield Vistas—Who Cares?" 24 *Jour. of Amer. Inst. of Planners* 158 (1958), 162–165.

[39] Motorist needs and services study, note 26 above, p. 19, observes that "the bunching phenomenon is based on the oil marketers' philosophy that competition is healthy."

[40] The most frequently cited studies are described in O. Kipp, "Final Report on the Minnesota Roadside Study," Highway Research Board Bulletin 113 (Washington, 1952), p. 33; J. McMonagle, "Traffic Accidents and Roadside Features," Highway Research Board Bulletin 55 (Washington, 1952), p. 38; A. Lauer and J. McMonagle, "Do Roadside Signs Affect Accidents," 9 *Traffic Quarterly* 322 (1955); "Relationship Between Accidents and the Presence of Advertising Devices," prepared for New York State Thruway Authority by Madigan-Hyland Inc. (mimeo, Feb. 9, 1963), reprinted in 109 *Congressional Record* 4578–4579, Mar. 25, 1963; R. Ady, "An Investigation of the Relationship Between Illuminated Advertising Signs and Expressway Accidents," *Research Review*, Mar. 1967 (Chicago: National Safety Council), p. 9.

tion is a potential hazard.[41] Studies of vehicle speeds on open stretches of rural highways show a steady annual increase in average speeds since World War II,[42] and studies of advertising signs show that larger signs are needed in order to convey advertising messages at these speeds.[43] So the highway engineer draws the inescapable conclusion: if we want highway efficiency and safety, roadside features have to be controlled.

The problem of designing highways which fit into their environment as integral rather than extraneous features is currently calling for a mobilization of many talents.[44] The results of better efforts in this direction will, hopefully, mean better selection of highway routes to minimize the disruptive effects of highway construction on surrounding land. Part of these efforts, however, will be directed to dealing directly with improving roadside areas through alignments, landscaping, and joint development of highways and highway-related facilities.[45] This new emphasis on the compatibility of road and roadside is in direct response to a public demand for planning the use of space so that it is used with economy and amenity. And, coming as it does after so many parts of American towns and cities have been allowed to develop into miles and masses of highway blight and clutter, there are some who fear that even this may be too late to correct these mistakes.

One final element of the interest which public agencies have in an accom-

[41] E.g., *Moore* v. *Ward,* 377 S.W.2d 581 (Ky., 1964); *Ghaster, Inc.* v. *Preston,* 200 N.E.2nd 328 (Ohio, 1964). See also testimony of Charles Fraser in *Proceedings of White House Conference,* note 1 above, pp. 275–276.

[42] Press release, Federal Highway Administration (FHWA-81), Nov. 29, 1967.

[43] Report of Ohio State University Research Foundation, 1959.

[44] E.g., the so-called "urban design concept" teams recently organized to study and recommend expressway route locations in Baltimore and Chicago.

[45] P. Lewis, "The Highway Corridor as a Concept of Design and Planning," in Highway Research Record 166, "Highway Corridor Planning and Land Acquisition" (Washington: Highway Research Board, 1967), pp. 1–8; *A Proposed Plan for Scenic Roads and Parkways,* prepared by U.S. Dept. of Commerce for President's Council on Recreation and Natural Beauty (Washington: GPO, 1966).

modation of roadside advertising and highway beautification relates to the governmental structure within which public programs are carried out. At present the major highway programs in the United States are carried on in the framework of a federal-state grant-in-aid system. In this federal-aid highway program, state highway departments build highways and the federal government shares in their costs, subject to the requirement that the state's planning, design and construction meets federal standards. This system has been carried on successfully for fifty years—since the Federal-Aid Road Act of 1916[46]—and its success may be attributed to an advancing technology, a system of taxation which has provided funds to undertake programs of continental dimensions, and a careful division of responsibility and power which has respected the roles of national, state and local government. In the highway beautification program, all three levels of government have a very basic interest in seeing that this balance is not destroyed. Proposals for the accommodation of roadside advertising and highway beautification, therefore, must be sought not only with the objective of finding ends that are equitable but also means that are consistent with the system through which they are to be implemented. In summing up, I would offer the following:

The organized, standardized outdoor advertising industry seeks recognition as a legitimate form of business, eligible to operate where other forms of commercial and industrial activity are located, with its property rights sharing in the same protection that American constitutional law gives private property in general. Understandably, also, it seeks to assure its future growth by preventing prohibition of roadside advertising along highways yet to be built. Many of the standardized companies and their clients believe their greatest interest is in keeping the urban areas open.[47]

[46] 38 Stat. 355, July 11, 1916.

[47] J. Cloonan, S. Gabis, and R. Goode, "Estimates of the Impact of Sign and Billboard Removal under the Highway Beautification Act of 1965," prepared for Missouri State Highway Commission (Columbia: University of Missouri, 1966), p. 29.

The unorganized segment of the outdoor advertising industry has basically the same interest, except that it is not so sure it can survive in competition with the organized group if its operations are limited to the commercial-industrial zones. This segment of the advertising industry, and the businessman-advertiser group that conducts its own advertising along the roadside, is interested in the land that is presently uncommitted by zoning or predominant commercial-industrial use and which someday will derive advertising value from future highway construction. These groups wish to have their chance to become established along the roadside before regulation is imposed or under any system of regulation that is established.

To a great extent the on-premise and off-premise business-advertisers who have established themselves adjacent to the highway, or who wish to do so, want the same thing—a chance to move into locations where they can reach the highway traveler through their outdoor signs. Unlike the national brands advertisers, who use signboards to gain the public's general identification and acceptance of their products, the highway-oriented businessman-advertiser feels he must concentrate on the traveler and win his patronage while he is using the highway.

Landowners of billboard sites have no obvious or well-defined interest in the question of regulation, for although they see that in some circumstances it may hurt the income they receive from renting their land, they also see that under other circumstances it may make their sites more valuable.

Owners of land in the vicinity of billboard sites and residents of the "neighborhood" naturally view their interest in terms of the economic impact that outdoor advertising and its regulation may have on their neighborhood land values. In addition, however, all communities seem to have a hard core of pride which has been expressed in the long history of regulatory controls on signboards by local governments and which evidences a general desire to reintroduce amenity where it has been lost in community development or to prevent the development of clutter in the local environment while there is still time to do something about it.

The highway user carries this same desire for more amenity and less clutter with him when he travels, and whether his trip is long or short, he tends to favor the places that favor the scenery or use good design in man-made facilities. At the same time that he resents the aggressive side of commercialism in outdoor advertising, he accepts and uses roadside signs to learn of and locate services he needs as he travels. Significantly, one of his chief complaints is directed against inadequate or confusing signs. He favors highway beautification as a goal; he believes he knows what he likes and dislikes when he experiences it; and he wonders why a sensible accommodation of roadside advertising and highway beautification seems to be so complicated for those who have the power to do something about it.

Those who have the power to do something about it—the governmental agencies responsible for planning, designing and managing the environment of the highway—have to take a long view of the public's needs. Costly experience with highways which have been rendered functionally obsolete prematurely by allowing unregulated roadside development has led them to call for control of the roadside as well as the roadway. The frustrating experience of finding that, despite the critical need for improving the transportation system, people (both urban and rural) sometimes rebel against having highways built in their communities, and would rather go without the convenience of such improvements than undergo the disruptive effects that follow their construction, has begun to make highway planners and designers aware of the need to think more carefully about the environment that is created by development of the land. The public's interest, therefore, is basically in prudent use of community resources by assuring that land development carried on through both the public and private sectors of the community is based on design standards that integrate the features of the environment in accordance with economy, convenience, safety and amenity or harmonious balance. Among these factors there is no priority, since experience has shown that in the long run all must be present or else all will suffer. Each supports the others in achieving an over-all general goal. Finally, because public agencies must exercise their powers within a framework of laws and governmental structure, these agencies have an interest in the way in which accommodations are to be accomplished, for the American federal system represents a deliberate balance of functions and responsibilities which must be maintained in order to be effective.

ACCOMMODATION: THE RANGE OF ISSUES

Comparing these interests and the positions which have been taken by the parties, what emerge as the critical issues that must be resolved?

First, it would seem that there is no real difficulty about the desire of the outdoor advertising industry, or the businessman-advertiser, or the landowner-lessor of a billboard site to be recognized as being just as legitimate a form of business as any other lawful form of commerce and industry. So far as I am aware, this proposition never has been seriously disputed. In consequence, all of these parties are entitled to the protection which the law gives property generally, and, also, each must accept the responsibilities which property owners have when their activities affect the general good. One of these obligations involves accepting regulation of one's activities when it is necessary to achieve the harmony of all interests.

*A Well-Known Animated and Illuminated
Outdoor Advertising Board*

Here, perhaps, is the first area of unresolved issues, for it is obvious that proponents of outdoor advertising and the rest of the community often hold different views of when and where the necessity for regulation exists. This difference often is the reason for such questions as: Should signboard control be applied to cities, suburbs and their approaches? And, should controls be directed at creating pockets of scenery or corridors of beauty? The premise of such questions, it has always seemed to me, is that control of billboards is for the purpose of promoting aesthetic considerations and that "aesthetic considerations are a matter of luxury and indulgence, rather than of necessity."[48] This was what American state courts said at the turn of the century, following what they understood the common law of nuisance had always held.

To argue the necessity of billboard control today in terms of aesthetics as luxuries and indulgences misses entirely the point of what is bothering Americans about the pattern of life that is developing and the way their communities are growing.[49] The question of necessity is now being viewed in a much wider context which seeks to relate land uses to their total environment. The concept of "highest and best use"—a term which zoning lawyers and condemnation lawyers have taken over and forced into a straitjacket of technical meanings—is acquiring a new relevance as the impact of land use on this total environment becomes better known. And, just as potential hazards of air, water and soil pollution have become factors in deciding to regulate land use, so pollution of the landscape is also relevant. This is implicitly conceded by the advertising companies' argument that they should not be regulated so long as there

[48] *Passaic* v. *Patterson Bill Posting Co.,* 62 Atl. 267 (N.J., 1905).

[49] N. Williams, Jr., "Legal Techniques to Protect and to Promote Aesthetics Along Transportation Corridors," in Highway Research Record 182 (Washington: Highway Research Board, 1967), 27. See also, W. B. Snow (ed.), *The Highway and the Environment* (New Brunswick: 1959) and C. Tunnard and B. Pushkarev, *Man-Made America* (New Haven: 1963).

are other land uses which are worse detractors of the landscape than they are.[50] Additionally, I think there is significance in the fact that when outdoor advertising controls have been tested in the courts, it has been planners rather than art critics who have been the most influential witnesses.[51] So, as one considers the necessity of regulating roadside advertising from the wider viewpoint of all the parties who have an interest in it, and as more becomes known about the potential impact on these interests, the premise that billboard control is a matter of luxury and indulgence becomes a relic of the 1900's. The ultimate accommodation of outdoor advertising and highway beautification thus calls for a new calculation—a policy decision—as to what, where and how much regulation is needed to protect the interests as they now appear.

One result of recognizing that this accommodation of interests involves more than merely a vendetta of garden clubs against billboards is that the area of accommodation cannot be focused on any one segment of the highway system. The rural mileage is as important in its way as is the urban and suburban mileage. Commercial district amenities are just as important as those of residential districts. Under such circumstances, proposals to concentrate control of roadside advertising in so-called scenic areas or along scenic highways wrongly assume that such areas and corridors are the only places where billboard blight hurts other legitimate interests.

The type and extent of regulation that is needed is also a major issue to be dealt with. Here necessity will have to be viewed in terms of varying circumstances. On Main Street, in the central city, and along the "gasoline alleys" of the suburban fringe, necessity would seem to require regu-

[50] E.g., testimony of Russell Robinson, Ohio Valley Advertising Co., Hearings, note 9 above, pp. 267–277.

[51] R. Barrett and R. Netherton, "Issues and Problems of Proof in Judicial Review of Roadside Advertising Controls," Highway Research Bulletin 337, (Washington: Highway Research Board, 1963), pp. 24–40.

lation of size, spacing, lighting and structural design of signs. This serves the interest of the advertiser in having some orderliness in the presentation of his message, and the interest of the neighborhood in providing some chance to develop or preserve whatever it can in the way of good design, privacy and amenity.

Along the open highway, the interests that the outdoor advertiser and highway traveler have in conveying and receiving information about travel-related services must be accommodated. But so must the interest of the highway department in preventing undue competition of commercial signboards with official traffic control and informational signs be accommodated. And so, also, must the joint interest of the traveling public and the general public in preserving the option for orderly development of the roadside areas. In a nation devoting one-third of its vehicle mileage to driving for social and recreational purposes, this objective of orderly development must necessarily include the appearance of the roadside.[52]

A regulatory system to accommodate all of these interests may well involve a division of responsibility for providing information to the highway user. For example, results of experimental systems of official signs, identifying brands and names of fuel, food and lodging services near interchanges of limited-access highways, indicate more motorist satisfaction with this method of publicizing fuel and automotive services than for food and lodgings.[53] This may suggest that official agencies might be relied on to provide information regarding automotive services needed to keep the motorist moving on the road, while commercial signboards might be relied on for food and lodging information.

Another facet of the accommodation appears in the current experiments

[52] Automobile Manufacturers Assn., *1967 Automobile Facts and Figures* (Detroit: 1967), p. 67.
[53] Interview with F. Thiel, Office of Research and Development, Bureau of Public Roads, Federal Highway Administration, Nov. 29, 1967.

with highway information centers. Often designed to operate in conjunction with highway safety rest areas, these centers provide space for advertising various types of services, features of interest to travelers and recreational facilities in nearby areas. In addition, maps and telephones frequently are available here to aid in selecting services. As such information-rest centers are established in greater numbers, and as motorists experience the advantages of freedom of choice and direct contact with the service facilities which these centers provide, dependence on roadside advertising may continue to decrease.

What ultimately emerges as a desirable division of responsibility between advertising signs and official informational signs and facilities will also be affected by developments in alternative sources of information. As these become more readily available, more imaginative and more personalized for the traveler's needs, the highway user is demonstrating his readiness to use them, particularly in selecting among a choice of services. And as the motorists' habits change, there is less and less basis for roadside advertisers to claim that off-premise advertising is essential to the traveler.

Public policy may be misguided by assuming that things will remain as they are or always have been. In the past twenty years this has been demonstrated dramatically by addition to the highway program commenced by the federal-aid legislation of 1956. Hopefully, the ultimate accommodation of highway beautification and outdoor advertising will take into account some of this research as it illuminates and evaluates the continuing validity of some of the premises on which present policy is based. In evaluating the future role of roadside advertising as against the goals of beautification, for example, I have already suggested that the steady increase in average speeds on open rural highways and the increased availability of alternative sources of information for the motorist are relevant factors. Some responsible opinion among advertisers even holds that the automobile—which brought outdoor advertising its greatest physical asset, the highway system—will ultimately engender technological and sociological advances that render billboards obsolete.[54] And it is just possible that the jumbo boards (four times the size of standard billboards, erected outside the 660 feet restricted area and visible for a mile) which have been going up in Iowa at the rate of one a week recently may be the dinosaurs leading the way to extinction of their breed, for surely their use by many advertisers is ruled out by costs.[55] If so, it would explain another current Iowa phenomenon, namely, use of roadside fields for parking large truck-trailer rigs with advertising signs on their sides.

When legislators face the need for an accommodation, they tend to compare what is to be gained in one direction with what may be lost in another. What ultimately is decided about highway beautification, therefore, may well be the result of balancing what we feel is gained in achieving a more agreeable environment against what we feel may be lost by having less information from roadside advertising for the motorist as he travels.[56]

[54] H. Gossage, "How To Look At Billboards," *Harpers Magazine,* Feb., 1960, p. 13.

[55] See, R. Netherton and M. Markham, *Roadside Development and Beautification: Legal Authority and Methods* (Washington: Highway Research Board, 1966), Pt. 2, p. 46.

[56] Missouri Highway Commission study, note 47 above, p. 20, containing the following observation:

> To a majority of travelers the value of information from roadside signs exceeds the value of the beauty lost by their existence. We have no measure of the margin by which the information worth exceeds the value of the beauty lost. At the same time we have 40% of the people to whom the beauty is worth more than the information. Faced with these inconsistencies one might infer that the value of the beauty to be gained by the elimination of signs and the value of the loss of information are about equal. . . .
>
> It seems a reasonable contention that in most instances, where there is a heavy concentration of signs, removal of some signs probably increases aesthetic value more than it reduces informational value. And conversely where there is a great sparsity of signs, the removal of a few signs probably contributes less to the aesthetic value than it detracts from the informational value to the traveler. Obviously these relationships will be quite variable and dependent on a number of local factors.

ACCOMMODATION: THE STRUCTURE OF
POLICY-MAKING AND ADMINISTRATION

In addition to issues regarding the need for control, and the type and extent of control, there is a question of who should be responsible for what in the regulatory program. I have already referred to the possibility that certain types of motorist information may be more effectively provided by private rather than public efforts. This approach should be explored not only in regard to *types of information* but also *types of information facilities*. For example, is there any reason why the advertising industry or a local chamber of commerce could not operate an information-rest area? Some state highway departments now contract with private industry for certain highway maintenance functions: toll road authorities rely on concessions to provide food, fuel, automotive services and rest facilities. Maybe there is a mutually advantageous division of labor in providing information needed by motorists.

Another aspect of the allocation of regulatory responsibility relates to the roles of federal, state and local governments in those matters which are decided to be public concerns. In 1958, one of the main arguments of the outdoor advertising industry and roadside businessmen against enactment of a federal law on billboard control was that this was a matter for local government.[57] Currently, I understand that, in negotiations to agree on standards for signboard control under the 1965 beautification act, these groups favor statewide standards rather than use of local standards.[58] In the 1965 federal law, which calls for negotiation of fed-

[57] Statement of Harley Markham, Outdoor Advertising Assn. of America, in U.S. Cong., Senate, Hearings before Subcommittee on Roads, Committee on Public Works, "Control of Advertising on Interstate Highways," 85th Cong., 1st Sess., Mar. 26, 1957, p. 301.

[58] Interview with James Billett, Assistant Chief Counsel, Federal Highway Administration, Nov. 30, 1967.

eral-state agreements on standards for size, spacing and lighting of permitted signs, "customary use" and the state's laws designating commercial-industrial zones are to be accepted for this purpose.[59] Under the 1958 federal legislation, national standards were promulgated by the Secretary of Commerce on these subjects.

Here, certainly, is an important element of any program for beautification and accommodation of the interests involved, and one where clarification is needed. From the states' viewpoint there is a certain natural uneasiness about the drift of policy-making power to the federal government, which they see as possibly being accelerated by federal promulgation of standards.[60] The mechanism of negotiated agreements provided in the 1965 beautification law at least contemplates state participation in the ultimate decisions on standards, although its initial administrative implementation did not appear to set up the same working relationship that has been followed in development of geometric and construction standards for federal-aid highways in the past.[61]

[59] Title 23, U.S. Code, "Highways," §131 (d) and (g).

[60] Although the Hayden-Cartwright Act of 1935 made federal participation conditional on the state's protection of its highway user tax revenues against diversion, and the Federal-Aid Highway Act of 1956 required states to apply the labor standards of the Davis-Bacon Act in their construction contracts, the most significant developments have occurred since 1962. The Federal-Aid Highway Act of 1962 barred federal participation in urban highway projects which were not based on certain planning processes in which state and local agencies had cooperated. This same act also required states to establish programs to assist in relocation of persons displaced by highway construction. In 1966 the National Highway Safety Act required states to carry out highway safety programs consistent with national standards as a prerequisite to receiving federal highway aid. And, of course, the 1965 Highway Beautification Act substituted a penalty approach for the incentive (bonus) approach used in the 1958 advertising control act.

[61] The Highway Beautification Act, passed in October, 1965, provided (§303) that public hearings should be held in each state before standards, criteria or regulations relating to advertising sign controls were promulgated. Pursuant to this, the Secretary of Commerce, in January, 1966, issued certain draft standards for consideration at these hearings (31 *Federal Register* 1162–66). Despite the fact that the drafts were explained

It is also a fair question to ask how far the states really retain a position of effective participation in policy-making and administrative authority under the 1965 law when Congress has prescribed the "customary use" approach to standards on size, spacing and lighting, and that compensation shall be paid for removal of existing signs.[62] Noting, but passing over, the question of whether it is financially practical for states to sacrifice 10 percent of their alloted share of federal highway funds by not going along with the federal policy decision in this matter, there are several purely legal difficulties that may have to be faced. One of these relates to the certainty which is offered by standards based on "customary use." It would be temptingly easy to say that this refers to the practice of the standardized outdoor advertising industry, but there is no evidence that Congress intended such a delegation of authority. If not, what benchmarks can one use in this matter? Some state law and a good deal of local ordinance law has been addressed to the subject of specifications for advertising signs, but its relevance to the environmental goals of the present and future is questionable. What, for example, does one do about jumbo signs designed to reach the highway from outside the regulated zone? What about the trailer rigs with advertising on their

---

as being "intended solely as guidelines for consideration and discussion purposes . . . and do not represent any conclusions, or even tentative conclusions, on the part of the Secretary of Commerce," the outdoor advertising industry and certain members of Congress objected that this action violated the intent of Congress by restricting roadside advertising too drastically, and that states might mistakenly assume these were the standards for the program. See *Congressional Quarterly,* Apr. 1, 1966, pp. 711–714, 720. Congressional hearings were scheduled in both House and Senate in the summer of 1967, and the question of administrative interpretation of the law was finally resolved by the Secretary of Transportation writing to the Chairman of the House Committee on Public Works assuring him that in negotiating agreements with states the federal government would accept state determinations of land-use zones, predominant land use, and customary use under state and local zoning. See U.S. Cong., Senate, Hearings before Subcommittee on Roads, Committee on Public Works, "Highway Beautification and Highway Safety Programs," 90th Cong., 1st Sess., June 28, 1967, pp. 1–12.

[62] Title 23 U.S. Code, "Highways," §131 (d) and (g).

sides parked in the protected zone? What about the laws introduced in a number of states (and passed in one or two instances) this past year which declared that all unzoned roadside land between municipalities was to be considered commercial in character? The point here is that in an effort to accommodate the outdoor advertising industry's interest in preserving its present methods of operation and assuring its future, the legislative draftsman may have made it more difficult to preserve a method of administration which has been successfully applied in the federal-aid highway program for many years.

The same thing may be said of the mandate that those states which remove signs must pay compensation to sign owners and landowners. At least one state, through its attorney general, has questioned whether this requirement can be implemented without violating the state constitution.[63]

As American society becomes more and more urbanized, the character of the American federal system is also changing from a two-level to a three-level structure, and a meaningful role for cities and counties must be worked out in the field of protecting environmental quality as well as in other fields of public interest. Local government's record in land-use control during the past twenty years has received criticism, and it has been suggested that a mechanism for establishing principles of land-use control and coordinating their application should be created at the state level.[64] This tendency to rely on state agencies rather than on local government has been particularly evident in suggestions for assuring orderly land-use patterns in areas near interchanges and developing the multiple

[63] Testimony of Delbert Johnson, Assistant Attorney General, Washington State Highway Commission, U.S. Cong., House, Hearings before Subcommittee on Roads, Commitee on Public Works, "Review of Highway Beautification—1967," 90th Cong., 1st Sess., Apr. 5, 1967, pp. 44–51.

[64] Babcock, note 18 above.

use potentials of highway corridors.[65] Unquestionably, it makes a good deal of sense, in every aspect except the political side, to try to establish the mechanism for developing the highway corridor area at the state rather than the local level. We discovered this fifty years ago when we started to develop highways as *systems* rather than *segments*. But highway beautification differs somewhat from the purely functional goal of building facilities for moving traffic, and local interests in the over-all result of these efforts on their environment are more deeply involved than in previous highway programs. An accommodation of highway beautification and outdoor advertising which does not allow these interests to be introduced into the decision-making process where they are affected is likely to be weaker than one that does.

One final area of matters which deserves major attention in outlining the range of possibilities for an accommodation of interests relates to the means used to achieve it. Aside from self-regulation, which I presume is ruled out by past experience and the basic difficulty of visualizing any organizational framework in which such an effort could be carried out, the choice of means centers around three of the most familiar powers of government—the police power, the power of eminent domain (including the power to make voluntary purchases) and the tax power.

Before looking into possibilities of using these powers in combination, it is necessary, of course, to evaluate the strong points and limitations

[65] Wisconsin Department of Resource Development, *The Protection and Development of Interchanges on Wisconsin's State Highway System* (Madison: 1961, multilith); D. Mandelker, and G. Waite, "A Study of Future Acquisition and Reservation of Highway Rights of Way," prepared for U.S. Bureau of Public Roads (Washington, 1963; U.S. Department of Commerce, Recommendations for Land Acquisition, Scenic Easement and Access Control for the Great River Road in Wisconsin (Washington: Bureau of Public Roads, 1963, multilith); Victor Gruen Associates, *Transportation Aspects of Land Use Controls*, prepared for NCHRP (Washington: Highway Research Board, 1966, multilith).

of each in its own right as applied to the goals of environmental quality. In this respect, use of the police power to restrict outdoor advertising in roadside areas is a familiar storm center to all who have read the literature of planning and zoning law. For the last seventy-five years, signboard owners have been in and out of court defending themselves against police power regulations by state and local government.[66] In the mass of precedents that has resulted there is something for everyone and, depending on the position one wants to espouse, there is a case that will provide the opening wedge for his argument.

I happen to believe that, under the recent decisions of the state courts, the limits of the police power are being interpreted broadly enough to allow state or local governments to go as far in restriction of roadside advertising by regulatory means as any responsible proposal is likely to require. Certainly I believe the states could implement the provisions of the 1965 Highway Beautification Act by their police power, as, indeed, many were doing under the 1958 law to control signs along the Interstate System. I think when five state supreme courts consider the constitutional questions involved and find no fault with the state's police power law there are grounds for this belief. I am aware that one other state, Georgia, has ruled that its state's highway department cannot remove billboards from roadside controlled areas without payment of

[66] A selection of articles on control of outdoor advertising over the past 50 years includes: C. Goodrich, "Billboard Regulation and the Aesthetic Viewpoint With Reference to California Highways," 17 *Calif. Law Rev.* 120 (1929); "Zoning — Control of Outdoor Advertising," 80 *Univ. Pa. Law Rev.* 120 (1932); C. Gardner, "The Massachusetts Billboard Case," 49 *Harv. Law Rev.* 869 (1936); A. Thompson, "Billboards and Zoning," 3 *Traffic Quarterly,* 348 (1949); Amer. Auto. Assn., *Roadside Protection* (Washington: 1951); Rodda, "Accomplishment of Aesthetic Purposes Under the Police Power," 27 *S. Cal. Law Rev.* 149 (1954); Highway Research Board, Special Report 41, *Outdoor Advertising Along Highways* (Washington: 1958); M. Price, "Billboard Regulations Along the Interstate Highway System," 8 *Kan. Law Rev.* 81 (1959); D. Johnson, "The Structure and Content of State Roadside Advertising Control Laws," Highway Research Bulletin 337 (Washington: Highway Research Board, 1962), p. 6.

compensation, but I cannot feel that this court, which spent its time castigating Congress for destroying states' rights and did not discuss the merits of the legislation beyond the single question of uncompensated removal, has really clarified the question for the rest of the country.

At any rate, if the limits of the police power on this matter of regulating billboards through zoning, or requiring removal of signs after a suitable period for adjustment and amortization of investment, is really in doubt, there is a clear constitutional question (and perhaps a divergency of state rulings) which can be taken to the United States Supreme Court, and those who feel that beautification proposals impair private property rights have access to this court.

So, I suggest that in accommodating highway beautification and outdoor advertising the police power is one of the chief means available to the states and that its use can be sustained at least to restrict signboards to only certain locations in roadside areas and, in those zones where they are permitted, to regulate such features as size, spacing, lighting and structural design. I suggest, also, that if it becomes necessary to extend the limits of protected zones from 660 feet to the horizon in order to deal with the jumbo signs, that step can be sustained. And I would also seriously consider the possibility that states might find it desirable to regulate the content of roadside signs to assure that those oriented to the motorist on the highway from a visual standpoint should also be oriented to his needs from an informational standpoint. For an activity which continues to justify its claim to a place at the roadside in terms of the service it performs for the highway user, this seems fair enough.

Zoning, of course, is prospective in its application and still leaves to be resolved the problem of removing signs that are not compatible with the plan of environmental design which is sought to be developed. As I read zoning law, however, I find no reason to believe that this problem of gradual elimination of nonconforming land uses cannot be solved

Advertising in the Public Interest

reasonably and fairly under the police power.[67] If there is a feeling that
we do not yet know enough about the use of the technique of amortization, then it is time to find out about it by trying it in various situations.
Certainly it appears to be one means of accommodating the economic
interests of advertisers and landowners with the interest of almost half
of the states and numerous cities and countries in their present systems
of land-use control.[68]

In this connection it is obvious that policy considerations should be
distinguished from legal necessities more clearly than they have been in

[67] C. Rhyne, *Municipal Law* (Washington: 1957) and cases cited therein.

[68] Babcock, note 18 above, has noted that the technique of eliminating nonconforming
uses "is at least two decades old, but the appellate decisions can be counted on your
fingers. The primary reason for the lack of litigation is that municipalities are so dubious
of the validity of this device that they hesitate to apply it if it will result in substantial
loss to the property owner. Consequently, amortization is typically applied only to signs
and temporary structures where the property owner does not have sufficient investment
involved to justify a legal challenge" (p. 98).

the past. Witness here the heated debate that has ensued over the provisions of the 1965 Highway Beautification Act which call for states to compensate sign owners and landowners for removal of billboards. Proponents of this requirement have claimed it is necessary under constitutional law. Opponents have said it is a policy decision taken to relieve anticipated hardship.[69] I believe legal research sustains the latter view. But the main point here may really be the one expressed in the old observation that "it weren't so much what he done, but the narsty way he done it." It is not a new thing for Congress to provide special relief for interests which might otherwise suffer unduly in adjusting to the highway program. In 1958 Congress amended the Federal-Aid Highway Act to authorize federal participation where states elected to pay the cost of relocating utilities due to highway construction.[70] In 1962, Congress similarly authorized participation in costs of relocating displaced persons and businesses where states paid these costs.[71] The cost of eliminating safety hazards at grade-crossings is a subject for negotiated federal participation instead of being put entirely on the railroads.[72] The 1958 law controlling outdoor advertising along the Interstate System authorized federal participation when states elected to acquire advertising easements.[73] On the merits of the hardships involved, these cases seem every bit as deserving as the cases presented by the advertising industry and billboard site owners. To the outside observer, therefore, it is hard to understand why national policy on compensation for removal of signs should not have been handled in this way. Or, for

[69] See, e.g., testimony of Dr. Spencer Smith, Citizens Committee on Natural Resources, Hearings, note 61 above, pp. 59–74 and Hearings, note 63 above, pp. 186–194.

[70] Title 23, U.S. Code, "Highways," §123.

[71] Ibid., §133.

[72] Ibid., §130.

[73] 72 Stat 89.

that matter, why compensation for removal of *visual access* to the highway should not be treated in the same way as removal of *physical access* to the highway, namely, a matter to be determined by state law. Yet in the 1965 beautification act, Congress imposed on the states a mandate to pay compensation in all instances.[74] By so doing it would seem to have ignored a basic interest of the states in maintaining the balanced relationship that has characterized the federal-aid highway program for fifty years and, in some states at least, to have substantially worsened the chance of achieving a successful accommodation.[75]

If mandatory compensation for sign removal remains part of the ultimate accommodation framework, it will take a while to fit it into the law, for on its face it does not go neatly into the concept of eminent domain or public land acquisition. For example, if we say this is a compensatory taking of property, what property interest does the state get for its money? A used billboard? An easement on an advertising site? An unexpired lease?

And, what principles of compensability and valuation apply? Should compensation be for the unused economic life of the sign? Or for the remaining years of a reasonable period of amortization? (This latter is an interesting suggestion from one state as to how police power and eminent domain may be combined.)[76] Should something similar to severance damage be recognized so that a sign company is paid for the effect on his total business of reducing the number of signs he operates? And if eminent domain principles are to be applied to compensation for billboards, what about the offset of benefits?

[74] Opinion of Hon. Ramsey Clark, Acting Attorney General of the United States, Nov. 16, 1966.

[75] Testimony of Delbert Johnson, Assistant Attorney General, Washington State Highway Commission, Hearings, note 63 above.

[76] See J. Kerian, "Valuation of Advertising Rights," Highway Research Record 166 (Washington: Highway Research Board, 1967), pp. 54–62.

These are some of the eminent domain questions which arise from insistence that an accommodation provide universal compensation. They may indeed justify the quip that the Highway Beautification Act deserves to be popularly named " The Lawyers' Twenty-five-year Full Employment Act." For myself, after twenty-five years' association with the law, I do not welcome more complications of this sort. I think there is room for more creative work by lawyers in exploring ways to combine use of public regulation and public acquisition in the field of environmental improvement. For example, in the creation of corridors for scenic, recreational and conservation programs, it has been suggested that initial regulation by zoning might protect the options of the public until the pattern of ultimate potential land use became clear. At that time the decision could be made as to what degree of public control should be continued, and acquisition of private property rights should be undertaken.[77]

Advertising in the Interest of Education

[77] J. H. Beuscher, "The Highway Corridor as a Legal Concept," ibid., pp. 9–13.

A few words should be said about the use of the tax power as a means for achieving accommodation. Actually a few words are all that can be said if one wishes to sum up experience with this technique, because little has so far been done in this direction. There is, however, much room for thought here, particularly as this means is being considered more extensively to induce private landowners to cooperate voluntarily with public encouragement of conservation, preservation of historical landmarks, open space and scenic enhancement.[78] Control of outdoor advertising is one among many components of the goal of over-all improvement of the environment. Combined with the other elements they all comprise a package which amply justifies the public expenditure (or abatement) of taxes. Why not see what it would cost to make it worthwhile for a landowner to exercise self-regulation of his own land?

There is, of course, another use of taxation, namely, taxing signs for the privilege of using the view created by the public highway. The legislative and judicial studies of roadside advertising which have occurred in the past ten years have given widespread publicity to the fact that outdoor advertising is "one of the most obvious nonvehicular users of public highways."[79] This has set people thinking, in particular about the status under property law of commercial advertising signs along the roadside. From this has come the suggestion that signs which are not part of some activity conducted on the land have no status as "property" (i.e., easements), but are simply a private use of the public highway.[80]

[78] E.g., *Workshop Manual of Conference on Scenic Easements in Action* (Madison: University of Wisconsin: December, 1966, multilith), pp. 31–35, 53–58; Urban Renewal Admin., *Open Space for Urban America,* prepared by Ann Louise Strong (Washington: GPO, 1965); Proceedings of Conservation Easements and Open Space Conference (Madison: University of Wisconsin, March, 1961, multilith).

[79] Third Progress Report, Highway Cost Allocation Study, House Doc. 91, 86th Cong., 1st Sess., Mar. 2, 1959, p. 53.

[80] R. Wilson, "Billboards and the Right to be Seen from the Highway," 30 Georgetown Law *Jour.* 723 (1942). See, however, references to the basis of this idea in *Churchill and Tait* v. *Rafferty,* 32 Philippines 850 (1915); *Perlmutter* v. *Greene,* 182 N.E. 5

The importance of this idea, as well as its applications to sustain the regulation of billboards under the police power, have been recognized by several state supreme courts.[81] And it is predictable that in the future the simple logic and morality of this proposition will give it an even more important role in policy-making. For certainly the application of this idea in tax policy is in keeping with the American article of faith that people should pay their own way in the economic world, and the policy of the Federal-Aid Highway Act of 1956 that the highway program should be paid for by its user beneficiaries.[82] As the current highway program comes under more and more pressure from higher construction costs and demands to add items which were not foreseen at its inception, it would be completely consistent for Congress and the states to turn to nonvehicular users of the highway for their fair share.

(N.Y., 1932); *General Outdoor Advertising Co.* v. *Department of Public Works,* 193 N.E. 799 (Mass., 1935) and C. Gardner, "The Massachusetts Billboard Case," 49 *Harvard Law Rev.* 869 (1936).

[81] This theory was used in *Kelbro, Inc.* v. *Myrick,* 30 A.2d 557 (Vt., 1943) as the basis for upholding police power regulation of signs. It was noted as a supporting factor in upholding the Interstate System billboard regulations in Ohio, Kentucky, New York, Wisconsin and New Hampshire. *Ghaster Inc.* v. *Preston,* 200 N.E.2d 328 (O., 1964); *Moore* v. *Ward,* 377 S.W.2d 881 (Ky., 1964); *People* v. *Schulman,* 176 N.E.2d 817 (N.Y., 1960); *Fuller* v. *Fiedler,* 120 N.W.2d 700 (Wis., 1963); Re: Opinion of the Justices, 269 A.2d 762 (N.Hamp., 1961).

[82] See, Federal Aid Highway Act of 1956, §209 (declaration of policy) stating: ". . . if it hereafter appears . . . that the distribution of the tax burden among the various classes of persons using the Federal aid highways, or otherwise deriving benefits from such highways is not equitable, the Congress shall enact legislation in order to bring about a balance of total receipts and total expenditures, or such equitable distribution, as the case may be."

Sec. 210 of this act directed studies to be made of, among other things, "any direct and indirect benefits accruing to any class which derives benefits from the Federal aid highways, in addition to benefits from actual use of such highways, which are attributable to public expenditures for such highways." 70 Stat 374, June 29, 1956.

This investigation was made in 1961, note 2 above, but Congress has not so far acted to tax nonvehicular beneficiaries to support the highway program.

CONCLUSION

If we are open enough in our thinking we will recognize that the accommodation must view highway beautification as part of a larger movement toward improvement of the total environment of our national community. Accordingly a wide range of interests are involved. And because some have not been as articulate and forceful as others in the past, our policy-making process may not have fully understood their full import.

If we take advantage of the variety of ideas that our society can generate, we will recognize the importance of the factor of changing times. Nowhere is this more evident than in the fields of transportation and management of the environment. To maintain the momentum of a great and vigorous continental community, we must appreciate the needs that are emerging, and if we do not meet them now, at least we must preserve our ability to meet them in the future.

And if we are wise we will not let our accommodation be based on expediency. Thomas MacDonald, who more than any other man deserves credit for our modern highway system, once said that we pay the price of good roads whether we have them or not, but the price is higher if we don't have them. So it is with accommodations—and, assuredly, in the long run we will pay a higher price if we rely on expedients.

INDEX